# Faces of Sickness…

# Faces of Sickness…

## Sick as $!*?

Second in the Powerful Series
"Eyes Wide Open, Mind Shut Tight"

*Tai Archbold*

iUniverse, Inc.

New York  Lincoln  Shanghai

Faces of Sickness…
Sick as $!*?

iUniverse books may be ordered through booksellers or by
contacting:

iUniverse
2021 Pine Lake Road, Suite 100
Lincoln, NE 68512
www.iuniverse.com
1-800-Authors (1-800-288-4677)

ISBN: 978-0-595-41458-1 (pbk)
ISBN: 978-0-595-85807-1 (ebk)

Printed in the United States of America

# Dedication

To everyone in my life that I love so dearly and to whom I may have been incapable of expressing just how much I cared, I thank you profoundly because it is through our soul dance that I was able to evolve to the level of understanding that I currently have. It is through our relations that I have been equipped to relate to others in such a magnificent way today. Thank you! My heart is filled with such an enormous amount of gratitude which is transformed into love for you and everyone I meet. I am not where I am going to be, but I am not where I was and I know that I could not have done it without you and your God essence. I hope that one day each and every one of you will be able to see and understand the ways of my love. I am so pleased that this journey that I am on is mine. The perfection of it leaves me enamored by how wondrous my Source is.

Love Always and Forever…And thank you.
*Tai*

# Acknowledgements and Credits

Special thanks to the individuals that made the vision of this book not only possible but tangible. I thank my editors Tanisha Morgan, Lisa Taylor-Huff, and Edna Morgan. These phenomenal women not only believe in me and my purpose, but they give their personal perfection to ensure its manifestation. Thank you to my children, who give proof that my beliefs work and I am so glad that they are benefiting so magnificently from them. And last but not least, to my grandmother Rose E. Davis whose unconditional love was the strength that nourished me. I am so blessed!

# Contents

# Introduction

Our relationships are the most meaningful parts of our lives. If we didn't have relationships with other people, would life even be worth living? Our relationships—whether with our parents, siblings, other family members, friends, coworkers, employers, neighbors, or even the clerk at the supermarket or the man who cuts your grass—are a direct mirror of who we are and who we are becoming. They all mirror parts of our personality. "If you spot it, you got it" (Colin Tippin) whether the trait be pleasant or unpleasant, if you spot it in others, you've got it in yourself.

As important as we know our relationships are to us, we also know that there are times when our relationships are just plain difficult. We don't understand why that neighbor is being so cranky today or why the boss exploded at that meeting. Sometimes we blame ourselves when our relationships don't go according to plan and sometimes we blame the other people involved. And, more times than we'd probably care to admit, we've made bad choices in our relationships.

I will expose you to information you can use to make sense out of your relationships. More than that: I want to help you create better, more fulfilling relationships with others and with yourself. This will improve your quality of life and have a positive "ripple effect" on the world. This is the reason I wrote this book, the second volume of the book series, "Eyes Wide Open, Mind Shut Tight".

I have taken bits and pieces of what others have shared with me from their experiences, as well as what I have lived and what I have seen, to create a vehicle by which I can convey a message that I believe to be very important for the success and less tumultuous completion of the journey on which we find ourselves. I thought that it would be highly effective to take true stories and fictionalize them so that they would get your attention. I wanted the stories to be informative so as to expose you to other levels of personal awareness, and also to serve as a base to introduce you to new ways for creating a better existence through learning new methodologies that you can implement. I know that if you allow it to, this book will assist you in achieving many of your desired life goals.

You will recognize yourself or someone that you know in these stories, and that's perfect. You see, the beauty of life is that all things are relative and there is nothing truly new under the sun. I always say, when God created the world, He said, "It is done"...not "It is done and I reserve the right to make changes". You need to know that everything that is brought into your consciousness is there for you to use. It is either a lesson or a blessing for you. Ultimately, everything that you are made aware of is a part of the process of developing you into who you are ultimately intended to be. It is part of the *emergence of "self"* process.

Read the stories, reflect on them, and see how you can use the knowledge from your reflection and your own experience to improve upon your current existence.

We are often taught things in an academic sense, such as in a classroom with textbooks and exams that test how well we have memorized the facts. The notion behind that practice is that we do this for preparation for later life. But the skills that would prove profoundly beneficial for functioning effectively in our present and future lives are not widely *taught*. Nor is there a standardized curriculum to prepare us for day-to-day living. We *need* "relationship training" from day one, and yet we are made to rely on the modeling and ineffective practices of the untrained people who are closest to us.

Here is my attempt at providing you with that training which you were not given earlier in your life. This book is designed to be a teaching tool to assist you now in the success of all your relationships.

My intention, as always, is to guide you in achieving a higher level of understanding of the beliefs to which you currently adhere. In addition, my intent is to offer new ways of being and doing things in your life that might be more beneficial so that you may better be able to apply the new information to your life. The key to mastering anything is understanding the concepts and being able to effectively apply the principles to produce the desired results. I believe that we have always had the keys to our successful mastery of this life. It is our unwillingness to learn how to use the keys and our resistance to using them that has inhibited us. We have been spewing the truth all of our lives without an understanding of what exactly it is we are saying.

Let's become aware. Let's realize that the awareness will only come by being exposed to something different—a new look at truth—and by being willing to consider the possibilities of what is. Remember, if it does not make sense, then it is nonsense: that is, *non-sense*.

Another helpful hint for you to remember is this: If you find yourself believing something just because someone else told you to, and you yourself don't have a personal understanding of that belief, ask yourself why are you defending the beliefs of another. No two people are the same and the beliefs you hold true must be true because of what they mean to *you* and what they represent in *your* life. Only then will those beliefs be "truth" for you. I'm not saying that you can not choose to believe what someone else believes; I'm saying that your beliefs should be based on *your* personal convictions, understanding, and practices, and that they must make sense to you. Remember this and you will find yourself operating from a place of personal alignment and not from personal division (being divided from your personal truth).

Think about it: if you were working at your job and some-one told you that certain rules were to be followed, but in practice those rules were not producing the expected results, you would not continue saying that they were effective. You would complain and then start presenting information to support what you have found to be effective through your experiences. So why would this practice not be applicable to your spirituality? *Stop just saying things because someone told you so.* If the wisdom does not produce the results, it's not effective wisdom and should be discontinued. "They will know you by your fruit". If what you're doing or saying is not producing results, something is wrong with the equation, and that's not rocket science. Again, I say, if it doesn't make sense then it is nonsense. And as long as it does not make sense to you, it won't produce desired results for you.

Let's make sense of this life so that we can understand the magnificence of our existence. We were created for relations with others. We are all connected and once we learn how to relate to each other more effectively, we will then join the dance of life. The resistance to our existence will dissipate and natural flow will take over and take us to a level of awareness where we will enjoy life and experience it more abundantly.

# 1. The Appetizer

The beauty of our existence is in our relationships. We were created to relate to and with things and other people. "We" in this context refers to the identity of who we are as the ego, not the essence of who we are as the collective Christ Consciousness.

At the core, all relationships are about the search for love. Yes, even your non-family, non-romantic relationships are about love. We all want others to like us and to accept us unconditionally. That's just another way of saying we want others to love us for whom we are on this journey.

The search for love is really the search for God. God *is* love, and when we look to share love with others, the ultimate desire that we seek is to be able to express our God Essence in the physical realm. If this concept seems foreign to you, you may want to explore the concepts and ideas expressed in my book *Take Five: The Five Minute Fix*.

Everything that happens in your life is there to train you for whatever is coming. Other humans join you in this process. Relationships are important because we use these individuals to help us achieve our goal of self-actualization. No matter how trivial you think a relationship is in your life, it serves a purpose. All of us are in the process of achieving the same goal, even though it manifests itself in different ways. Spiritual unfolding is what our current existence is all about: the surpassing of the **Ego Presence** to expose the **Spiritual Essence**. The trials and tribulations of living are part of the necessary process to manifest this end. This is the alchemy process, a process of changing something from its current state to release the true valuable presence. It was always there but in a state that was difficult to appreciate and value. The process, like changing ore into gold, is never completely done. You can change ore into gold bars that can be made into jewelry, and then the jewelry can be melted down and transformed into yet another beautiful form. It can be an ever changing and ever evolving process, and how magnificent is that! The possibilities are endless, and that is what we need to take notice of. The possibilities are unlimited because *we* are unlimited. Allow your self the space to experience the things necessary to be transformed. Relationships are the arena or the lab that facilitates this transformation.

It's about relating to one another. An effective relationship requires personality integration of the two individuals involved. It is the mutual agreement of both parties to engage in certain practices and to avoid others. The success of the agreement are greatly contingent upon the cooperation of all involved. Every relationship has "ground rules", whether spoken or unspoken. The question is, are the ground rules working well for both parties, or not?

Remember that you create your reality by the choices that you make. The outer vision of your world is exactly what you created. No matter how difficult you believe the choice was, *you* made it. There is always an alternative—whether you admit it or not. There is always another way. The best recommendation that I can make and one that I guarantee will produce successful results is for you to make decisions from a place of love as opposed to a place of fear. Fear-motivated choices will render consequences that will dissatisfy you for a long time to come. When you make love-motivated choices, those choices will *reward* you for a long time to come. The environment that you create with the choice motivated by love will always reward you favorably. Because it was created in love, it creates a loving peaceful place within in you that will allow you to feel powerful and self-assured.

Making decisions from a place of love seems difficult—especially when another person is acting out of fear and anger—because most times it goes against the status quo and requires courage, self-control, and a spirit of faithful knowing. Decisions made from a place of fear are easier because they seem to give immediate gratification; but that brief gratification diminishes quickly and you are left with such dissatisfaction that you feel as though your life is a total mess and not worth living.

If you don't like what you see, change the way you look at it. Realize where your current practices are *not* giving you the results you desire. Choose to always make love-based decisions regardless of how difficult they may seem, because the fear that you experience is only the guardian at the threshold of your blessing. No longer allow yourself to be an accomplice with your flesh to impede your progress.

If you can't be yourself and show your potential partner who you are and still be accepted "as is", you are not in a relationship best suited for you. If you are not able to grow, and the other person is unable to grow, and you are *both* unable to grow together, then the purpose of the relationship is simply to prepare you for relationships to come. Bless the relationship as such and be grateful for the experience. Then, look to the future with expectancy, for it is coming—never doubt. Source makes no mistakes and will never prepare you without having a purpose. Be still and know that He is God, or whatever you call your Higher Power.

All relationships seek a childhood connection. We either seek what we desired as a child or what we had as a child. We all desire to be close to others in some capacity. We all desire to be loved, and we all want to share some aspect of ourselves, if not our whole lives, with others. Desire is of God and the desire is there too because it is a natural urge that Spirit instills to guide you toward Source. Spiritual connection is the desire and we are drawn to others because we are the same; all one of the same Source, all a part of the same whole.

We want to know the meaning of life. What is the purpose of life? Here it is, simple and uncomplicated: Life is living the experience of moment-to-moment awareness of abundance and wonder. Your relationships are tools by which you are to become aware of the wonders of life and living. Be thankful for the experiences of each. And whether you believe them to be good or bad, what will be revealed to you are great wisdom and a sense of knowing. This will be a knowing that will grant you a perfect peace, one that surpasses all understanding. This kind of peace comes from the knowledge that what we believed life to be in our egos is, in fact, not that way at all. But instead, is an illusion designed to create darkness, an opportunity so that we will seek, discover, and display our light. When that happens, you truly experience the full purpose of life. You will feel it in your very being. Stop focusing on the distraction of the exercise and marvel in the results of the accomplishment.

The light of the world is you and me as our Essence and the more we allow our light to shine, the brighter, more powerful, and magnetic we become.

## 2. Sickness Attracts Sickness

It's not my favorite place. The walls are colorless, there's metal everywhere, it's eerily quiet at times and people are always peeking at me, sometimes whispering and then walking away. Still, I keep coming back. Despite how cold and sterile it is at times, I feel a certain amount of comfort here.

"Here's some information for you, Ms. Maynard. Read it over and see if you have any questions. I'll be back in a moment."

"Oh, sure. Thanks," I responded, taking the pamphlet the doctor was handing me. As he left the room, I started thumbing through it to see what the specifics on this STD were. *Swelling, itching, sores, yadda, yadda, yadda. Treatable. Good.* What I liked about this clinic was that it was open 24 hours and used volunteer doctors. That made it easier for me to get in and get treated without having some regular doctor judging me. *So I like sex. Who doesn't?*

I admit, I'd been doing some exploring since my ex and I separated five years ago. He had been my first and only lover and our love life had been so restricted: kisses on the neck, rubbing the booty, some dry humping, then missionary until the job was done. That's how it happened every single time, from the night of my Sweet Sixteen to the pity sex I gave him on his 33rd birthday three weeks after we'd finalized the divorce. To this day, I don't know why I felt pity for him. He was the one who was lacking in bed. It wasn't my skills or my weight like he'd always said. *He* was the problem; it took me a year and a half of therapy to be able to say that. He was the problem. It wasn't until I started meeting men here and there that I realized that.

"What's going on with you?" The doctor asked stepping back into the room. "Seems you've been here a number of times in the last fifteen months," he probed.

I looked up slowly from the brochure, composing myself and coaxing my best polite smile to shine through my surprise that he knew I'd been there before. *Did I forget to change my last name this time? No, he called me Maynard not Benjamin.* "I'm sorry you must have me confused wi..."

"Not likely that we'd have multiple patients in here with identical first names and last digits of social security num..."

"I said I haven't be..." I began.

"...bers. You just don't strike me as the type to be having these kinds of problems. If I didn't know better, I'd think you held a pretty decent job and you're certainly mature enough to know how to prevent things like this from happe..."

"You're right Doc," I interrupted, raising my voice slightly. "I'm not some silly coed. And I don't take well to lectures. So if you could just hand over the prescription I..."

"Yeah, well," he began while handing me the prescription, "it's your life. Keep making it hard for yourself if that's what you want to do."

I watched the door swing shut as the doctor left the room then I hopped off the table to get dressed. I slipped on my fishnets, my tweed Lane Bryant skirt suit and my Aldo Mary Janes and headed over to the mirror to fix my girls. *Lord knows he didn't give me all these breasts to hide under a suit.* I reached for my purse and dug out my make-up bag to do a touch-up. *That doctor doesn't know what he's talking about. Life is good. I've calmed down a lot over the last year. Especially since Marcel and I started getting serious. I stopped messing with Karen's husband Kyle months ago and I was clean the last time Marcel and*

*I went to the swinger's spot…I only messed with Michael a cou-*
*ple of times after that swinger's party and he was clean. He had*
*to have been if he was there…Sean and I only got together once*
*and he definitely looked healthy. I've certainly done all the right*
*things. My life is fine. I haven't been here that many times; just*
*once in September, then there was March, twice in June,*
*today…that can't be right.* I stopped midway through refresh-
ing the liner on my left eye and peered into the mirror. That's
when it hit me. *I never had anything serious happen to me until*
*I started messing with Marcel…a pregnancy or two that I*
*needed an emergency contraceptive for but never an STD.*
*Marcel…Marcel's trifling butt. Probably still running after frail,*
*twenty-something skanks. Got to be. That was the cause behind*
*the last STD I had. Happened three, no two days before Chris*
*Jr.'s 8^{th} birthday. Sure 'nough 'cause I was late picking up his*
*cake on account of my detour home to chew Marcel out.* "That
whole night was a funky mess!" I said aloud, studying my
reflection as I began replaying the incident in my mind.

"Where are you?" I screamed, slamming the door behind
me and beaming my keys onto the sofa. "Marcel…Bring yo'
a…"

"Woman, what's wrong wit you? You outta yo' damn
mind," he asked strolling into the living room. He was dressed
in his usual ensemble: tube socks pulled up to his knees, Phat
Farm jogging pants three sizes too big, a wife beater, a glass of
red Kool-aid in one hand, his brush in the other.

"You…you promised me and…I don't even believe you.
Are you trying to kill me?" I shouted throwing a half sheet yel-
low paper at him. "Herpes. Yo' cheating ass gave me Genital
Herpes this time."

"Rayna, now you know I haven't be…"

"What I know is that you can't freakin' do right. You're a
sick, twisted jerk. You know that? Twisted. All I do for you and
you still can't act right?"

"Rayna, calm down. What's your problem?" he asked, brushing his hair and plopping down on the sofa.

"You running 'round here charging up crap like you pay the bills—credit card, cell phone, speeding tickets on the Mustang…"

"Now, Rayna, you know I never asked for any of that. You put me on all those accounts and the car, well that was a gift. I mean…"

"What about the house I bought us, Marcel? What about that? You haven't paid a lick on it since we bought the damn house. And now I gotta pay for freakin' suppressants for the rest of my life too. This has been the worst six months of my life. I want you outta my house."

"I'm not goin' anywhere. This is my…"

"Be gone when I get back!" I snatched my keys off the sofa, got to my car as fast as I could and peeled out the driveway. As I hit the first stoplight, I fished my cell phone out of my purse to call my friend Dominique and vent. I told her what had happened and as usual, she didn't waste anytime lighting into me. In the midst of her reprimanding, another caller clicked in. Appreciative for the break from being scolded, I clicked over. Before I could even say "hello" the woman on the other end had started cussing me out, claiming that not only was she pregnant with Marcel's baby but that *she* was his fiancé. Before I could interject a few choice words of my own, the line went dead. I hung up with Dominique and dialed Marcel's cell. He picked up on the ninth redial.

"Rayna, are you crazy blowin' me up like that?" he shouted.

"Naw, you the crazy one. You livin' in my house…," I began.

"Our house; my na…"

"…and you had the nerve to not only sleep with some-one…or *someones* is probably more like it…and go get the chick, who's calling me talkin' 'bout *she's* your fiancé, preg-nant? You were supposed to be packing up the rest of your stuff in Cleveland, moving everything up here. You was packin' all right, huh. How many fiancés do you have? How many of us did you propose to, huh? What's that about, Marcel? What the......"

That was as far as the argument went because after that my attention turned to the black Escalade skidding towards me on the right and the oncoming traffic I'd swerved in front of trying to avoid it. It ended up being a bad accident, not a bunch of injuries just a lot of car damage. Still it was bad enough to knock me out for a while. When I came to, I remember thinking about how thankful I was to be alive so I could see my kids again and I truly believed that God had kept me alive to really live life; you know, do things right by my children and Marcel.

"God! How freakin' naïve was I?" I shouted at my reflection in the mirror, as I remembered what I'd been through already, all because of Marcel. And now *this!*

"Ma'am?" I heard a voice call out through the clinic exam room door, "Are you okay in there?"

"I'm fine," I replied, still looking in the mirror. *Mr. Marcel. You had me but not anymore. My nose is closed and it's going to take an act of the devil himself for you to sweep me off my feet again.* I finished up my eyeliner then grabbed my purse and headed to the car. The pharmacy was on the way home so I decided to stop to have my prescription filled. As I was driving I kept going over the past couple of months with Marcel in my mind and every time I replayed that day I got angrier and angrier. *The blinders are off you bastard.* As I pulled into the pharmacy parking lot, again, there was no doubt in my mind that I had misread that whole incident. God was nowhere up in there that day, at least not when it came to my and Marcel's relationship. The mastermind behind that had to have been the devil. *I'm going to have a chat with Don Juan Marcel again. But this time, if he doesn't fess up and straighten up, he's out on the street for real.*

"Hi Ma'am," the pharmacy assistant said as I pulled up to the drug store drive-thru window.

"Afternoon. I'd like to have this prescription filled. You should have my insurance information on file." The pharmacy assistant looked at the prescription then peered over her half glasses at me.

"What's the name and number?" she asked, her hands hovering over her keyboard.

"Rayna. Rayna Benjamin, 973-555-3-2-8-7," I replied.

"O.K. Ms. Benjamin. It'll be ready in about two hours."

"Great. I'll be back to pick it up then." I replied, picking up my cell phone. *Two hours is just enough time for a lunch quickie with Michael. Or better still, Lionel. An eye for an eye, Marcel.*

## Analysis

The first thing that we must become aware of is that as humans, and because of the purpose of life, we attract to us people and circumstances that reflect where we are in our evolution. What that means is that the people in our lives are there to serve as a mirror to ourselves, to assist us in our alchemy process, the transformation from our ego to our essence. We are all blessed and we are tested through the people in our lives. The people that you draw to you, you attract because of the choices you make. The choices you make create the situations in which you find yourself, and therefore the surroundings and people who inhabit your reality. Association does not truly bring on assimilation; it just allows for assimilation. Because we are spiritual beings we encompass every aspect of consciousness, that includes all things good and bad; and then we make the choice as to which characteristics we will demonstrate on a daily basis as part of our chosen character.

Rayna, in an attempt to explore other avenues of life, has placed her body and therefore herself in a position of danger.

She suffers from what I call "the grass is greener" syndrome. We look in our yard and see weeds, and then look in the neighbors' yards and see beautiful grass. We know why we have weeds in our yard, but we can only guess as to why our neighbor has beautiful healthy grass. And we want what the neighbors have. The problem with guessing how or why someone has the success you want is that you may find yourself with wrong information and as you know, one missing ingredient can mess up the whole dish.

Rayna was dissatisfied with her first relationship where she probably felt as though she was doing what she was supposed to do to create success according to society's standards, and yet she found herself in a failed union. So she decided that if what she had been doing was not getting her the success she wanted, she would do the exact opposite. She rationalized to herself that the "new" way would be more fun or at least more liberating. The issue here however, is that neither plan is rendering her the results she desires. She is obviously ashamed of the results of her actions because she feels a need to conceal her identity. She exhibits anger to her partner, blaming him for her current situation. Anger stems from fear of being harmed and a sense of helplessness. Yet, she continues to allow herself to stay in a situation that she knows is harmful.

Why would someone do that, unless she thought that she truly had no other options or that she was afraid to change? When someone stays in a situation that they perceive to be less than they want, it is because they feel that either they do not deserve better or that "better" does not exist. Both reasons are erroneous and should be eradicated.

You will find that we tend to gravitate to people who reinforce whatever opinions we have of ourselves. When I say that, I mean the opinion that we *really* have of ourselves, not the one that we *say* that we have—because they can often be two completely different things. Rayna probably felt that she lacked skills in the bedroom since her husband had been the only man that she had ever been with. She wondered if that was her husband's opinion, too, and used it to support her own insecurities. She felt uncomfortable about her weight and allowed her husband to use her insecurities about it to further validate the other negative feelings she had about herself and her relationship. She says that sexual promiscuity is wrong when someone does it to her, but proclaims it to be fun when she is doing it to someone else. If you don't like something when it is done to you, why would you do it to someone else? That's a double standard, and yet it happens more times than not.

People seeking intimacy will very often substitute sex for the experience of true intimacy. Sex has and is being misused, and because it is being used improperly, the full effect is missed. In an attempt to prolong or sustain "artificial intimacy" through sex, people "pervert" the intended sacredness of the physical union between man and woman. Then, because they don't get the intimacy they seek, they look for more sex to replace what they *really* want. It's like throwing the good after the bad and it just does not work. You will never be able to turn *up* into *down*. Basic principals and natural laws will apply and will never fade because they are truth and truth is relentless and unchanging.

The trick to getting what it is that you desire is to be true to yourself. Become open and present to your inner guide, your God Essence, and you will find that whatever it is that you seek, you will see. Notice that I said "see" and not "find". That is because nothing that you desire is *lost*. The reason that you are unable to see it is not because it does not exist, but because you refuse to become aware of its presence and acknowledge its existence.

Everything in your current reality is there because of the choices that you made and you made the choices because of the beliefs and fears that you had at the time. If you abolish the fears and make different choices, your reality as you know it will miraculously change. You draw to you the experiences in your life to teach you and take you to the next level. Be thankful for the experiences and see them for what they are.

And remember: *you are not the victim in any situation.* When you feel like a victim, know that you are really just a "student"—someone with something to be learned. Know that if you think that something or someone in your life is "the bane of your existence", that thing or person is there because you called it. Hence, *sickness attracts sickness*: you call to you whatever experience you need in order to teach and prepare you for the next level, and the experiences will continue to be called until you get the lesson—and subsequently the blessing. You call forth these lessons by the choices you make. And based on your choices, the lessons are necessary ones to help you deal with the reasons you make those choices.

So, if you don't like the outward picture of the people and the situations in your life, stop blaming others. Instead, look at yourself and start operating from a different perspective. "The men/women in my life are not giving me what I need." Well, you chose them or allowed them into your life. If you don't like it, revoke their guest pass and remove that type of person from your guest list. Problem solved. You see, everyone is on their own specific journey and your paths will only cross if your particular journeys collide in some way. When you are no longer on parallel journeys, those individuals will disappear from your life or from that segment of your life. People need each other. We use one another to come into and reveal our unique purpose. We aid and assist each other. When we no longer need each other we release one another to elevate and evolve.

The better plan of action for Rayna would be for her to stop and reflect on what it is she desires. She would need to know who she is—Ego or Essence—and what the true purpose of her life is. She would do well to know that we are not here to suffer or to judge or to be judged, but to express the beauty of life through our existence, and that the only thing that creates pain is our believing that we can be hurt.

The way to intimacy is to be vulnerable and present. The way to achieve that is by realizing that no one and nothing can really hurt you because you are not your body but your essence. Therefore, the experiences that you have are blessings, not punishments. Your experiences are designed so that you can see what you like and what you don't like and the best way to achieve the things that you do like. Life experiences will demonstrate your power to allow or not allow the things that are in your life. The way you exercise this power is to know what motivates you to make the decisions that you make.

Every decision is motivated by love or fear. Decisions made in fear are false and will ultimately lead you where you don't want to be, forcing you to find your way back to where it is you do want to be. "I'm with this man that cheats on me. I don't like it. I'm sick and tired of the lies and deceit." But you stay because you are afraid to be financially uncertain or alone. But why would you be financially uncertain? *You* don't provide for you. God does. Why would you ever be alone when you draw exactly what you need and desire to you when you are ready to receive it? When you look to a romantic partner to provide for you, you will be disappointed because that person, like you, is on a journey of self discovery. If they are on their journey, you can't predict what their actions will be, because they are constantly evolving into who they are purposed to be. We are all on a journey from our humanity into our Essence, and in the Essence, which is God, there is consistency and unchanging resolve.

Take a stand. Believe and know that you are worthy of whatever it is that you desire. But to get what it is that you long for, know that you must become that thing to yourself *first*. If you want to be loved, love yourself first. The things that you desire for others to do for you, do for yourself. If you want someone to respect you, make sure you respect yourself. If you want someone to admire you, find a way to admire yourself. If you want someone to spend quality time with you, spend quality time with yourself. If you want someone to treat you well, treat yourself well. Only allow the things that make you feel good and at peace in your space and watch how your life will change. Just as sickness attracts sickness, peace and happiness attract peace and happiness.

# 3.   Down Low Fo' Sho'

I was in no mood to talk to anyone when I got back to the house so I quickly ducked into the dining room, gave my hugs and kisses, and excused myself for the evening, blaming my early retirement on a 7:30 a.m. breakfast meeting. I was still concerned about work and even more so about why Tess wasn't. And on top of that, I was trying to sort through my relationship issues.

I went straight for the closet when I got to the bedroom to pick out my clothes for the next day. I hung up the suit jacket and put the dress shirt I was wearing into the "to be dry cleaned" pile in the corner. Then I surveyed my wardrobe. My eyes settled on my "power suit" section then reached for the suit I'd been eyeing. *Yup. Gotta be the Armani.* I laid my black pinstriped Armani suit, an Indigo Blue shirt and my Dusty Gold tie on the chaise in the bedroom sitting area. Though I felt strangely calm, my mind was racing. All I wanted to do was sleep but I knew I was due for a shave. So, I headed into the bathroom. I trimmed my mustache and eyebrows, then lathered up and began shaving. I nicked myself four times, something I hadn't done since I was seventeen years old. I was motionless as small droplets of blood formed on my chin and cheeks. *What are you doing Warren? This is not you. This cannot be you.* Right then, as I looked into the mirror and saw a bloodied man peering back at me, my mind began replaying the earlier events of the day...

The day, like most, had started out perfect. My wife's tongue was my alarm clock. I felt soft flecks on my nipple followed by piercing nibbles. She began kissing me on my ear, my neck, my jaw and then finally my lips. I knew what she wanted and despite the fact that I hadn't opened my eyes yet, I certainly was awake. I reached for her waist and pulled her close to me.

The sex was sensational. Morning wake-up call sex always was. After a few moments of after-glow, Tess kissed me on my cheek then tapped me on the back—her usual sign that she was ready for me to move. I rolled over onto the bed. She put her robe on, and said, "Breakfast in 20, okay?" and walked out.

Since we were both on a post-sex adrenaline high, I figured breakfast would be a good time to break the news to her about the specifics of the merger. She knew there was a merger pending, but that was about it. I'd known for weeks how much it could affect our family and I'd even tried to figure out a way to not tell her. You know, make things okay without worrying her. But I had been stressed and at a loss for solutions for weeks so I knew I had to tell her eventually. I figured today was as good as any.

After showering, I headed downstairs and out to the poolside patio for breakfast. Giara (the live-in help) had made a Denver omelet, hash browns and fresh squeezed Papaya juice for me, and Tess was sipping on her green tea. The kids were finishing their stuffed waffles while chattering away as usual: Donavan, about his dire need for a 525 for his 16th birthday; Paula about how her life would be over if she didn't go on the 8th grade French class summer trip to Paris; and Chris about me outfitting and sponsoring his whole little league team this year. To my surprise, Tess chimed in lobbying on their behalf, which I definitely didn't expect. I didn't think she was serious, but turns out, she was.

Right after Giara left with the kids to take them to school, Tess started laying on the guilt trip, saying that I'm never home and the least I could do was buy the kids what they need to soothe them. I just sat there, dumbfounded. I couldn't believe her—especially after that long chat we had over dinner last week about our finances and the challenges I'm having at work. Not to mention the one just yesterday: she and I sat down with our contractor who told us that the upgrades she'd ordered for our second home in South Beach were going to cost another $400,000. That would've been fine if I knew how things were going to pan out with the merger at my job, but obviously there's no way for me to know that. In her defense, I hadn't told her the specifics of the merger, so she didn't know that there were potential problems. I guess I should have clued her in about everything sooner and maybe she wouldn't have gone crazy on the tiles, countertops, fountains and whatnot. But still, you'd think the woman would slow down on the spending when our accountant, contractor and broker started having interventions with us.

So right about when she was riling off reasons why Paula should get to go on her trip, I just blurted it out: "My job's in jeopardy." She didn't say a word. I waited for her to process what I'd just said, expecting her to say, "Honey, how? Why?" or ask me if I was okay, give me a hug, you know, offer some sort of comfort. I got nothing. She just sipped her tea and sat silently. I took that as my cue to go on so I told her that there were bound to be changes and I was concerned. That was as far as I got though because at that point, she just cleared her throat, got up kissed me and said she was late for her appointment. She left me sitting there, staring at my own reflection in an empty plate, to figure out for myself how to deal with this situation. I must have sat there for fifteen minutes, just staring.

Eventually, I left to go to the office but once I got there, I was really just going through the motions of working. My mind wasn't even close to being focused on the project I was managing so I did what I always did: I called Barry for a game of basketball. I knew that I could talk to him and he'd comfort me and help me figure things out. Barry was in pharmaceutical sales and worked on his own schedule, so he was always game to play hooky. We met up at the half court on the rooftop terrace of his condominium complex and played some one-on-one.

It wasn't much of a game. I lost by six, which meant that dinner was on me. We had Chinese delivered to his condo; Moo Goo Gai Pan for him, General Tso's Chicken for me, and a quart of Fried Rice for us to split. We ate by candlelight then I headed to the shower to relax. Water always relaxed me and the shower was my thinking spot. I stood there letting the water massage my face and chest. *What am I supposed to do? What am I doing? Why does everything have to be so complicated? I never in my life thought I'd be in this situation. Never.*

A cool draft skated across my back and I felt the hair on the back of my neck stand up. *I was hoping for some company.* Instinctively, I reached behind me and pulled Barry close to me. He reached up and began massaging my head. I let go of his waist and turned around. He sank to his knees in front of me. With the water cascading off my chest and splashing down onto his face I let go of the thoughts plaguing my mind and focused on the pleasure of the moment.

I left the foggy bathroom and plopped onto the bed, letting the cool air from the fan above dry me off. I was physically refreshed but with adrenaline levels returning to normal and blood free-flowing in my body once again, the reality of my situation stormed back into my head. I had been trying to get past what had happened with Tess earlier in the day, but the more I thought about what happened and what had been happening with us, the more frustrated I got. So I did what I always did when I felt overwhelmed with life…I opened up to Barry. I updated him on the situation at work and rehashed everything that had happened earlier in the day from the pitch of her squeals during the wake-up call sex through her untimely exit at breakfast.

"She just up and left?" Barry said, poking his head out from the bathroom.

"Yes, she did," I replied. "And for a Botox injection at that."

"So what's her deal, Warren? Is she touched in the head from taking in all that Botulism toxin and saline?" Barry asked sarcastically.

"That's my wife you're talking about," I responded dryly as I got up to take in the view.

"Sorry. You know I adore Tess but really, why do you think she responded like that this morning?"

"I haven't the slightest," I said leaning my back against the window and facing Barry. "Sometimes it's like she becomes someone else; a stranger with no concern for anyone but herself, you know? It's not always like that but lately, I never know."

"I don't know how you do it, man," he said coming into the bedroom. The candles had burned down to nubs and now with the bathroom light out, I could barely see him; just the whites of his eyes and perfectly aligned teeth were visible.

"Love. Plain and simple. No matter how caught up in her own world she acts sometimes, I know she loves me and I still can't help but love her," I responded, gazing out at the Atlanta skyline. Barry had floor to ceiling windows in his condo so the view was spectacular. During the day, I could see for miles and even spot my own house when the skies were clear.

"Right. Crazy love. That's why I have no intention of letting myself fall any harder for Jackie than I already have," he said, pulling his towel from around his waist and throwing it onto the floor.

"It's a losing battle, my friend. Love conquers and commands all," I said, mesmerized by the lively city below me.

"Riiiiiight," he said plopping down onto the bed. I watched Barry's reflection as he got situated under the covers. As usual, he fluffed each of his pillows three times then flipped the top one over—he always had to have the cool side up. "So, back to your issue," he began. "If memory serves, best case scenario is that you keep your position and just have to deal with new rules, new superiors and a sh** load of extra work, right?"

"Right."

"And if the worse case does happen, which it won't, by the way, since we both know that your track record is way better than Isleman, Igerbaum, or whatever the dude's name is that's the Milovic Investments counterpart. But if the worse case happens, you'll still have a job but a different title, right?"

"Yes, but there's more to it. If *Ibersom* stays on, I'll end up working under him as part of his team for the Southeast and I'll likely have to take a 20% pay cut and…"

"And you're concerned you won't be able to keep up with the Jones," he chimed in trying to complete my sentence.

"Actually, I was going to say the Pierces."

"Warren, that's ridiculous. Your family loves you and will accept whatever lifestyle changes they'd have to make if, and that's a huge if, *if* you got demoted. Your wife, though she may have some withdrawal, would just reschedule the liposuction, breast realignment or whatever she has scheduled next to be 'fixed'. Donovan, I'm sure, would settle for a 3-series. Get Chris jerseys instead of full uniforms and his team will love you forever. And Paula, sweet Paula, you know a $500 gift card to Lenox Mall would put that pouting lower lip right back in place after she found out her trip was a no-go. So stop worrying."

"But the house in Miami…"

"Have the contractor put a hold on all the extras," he cut in. "Build the house as planned and if worse comes to worse, put it on the market as soon as it's done. You said yourself, the land appreciated $125,000 since you bought it two years ago. So that'll be some extra cash for you."

"You're right…"

"I know this," Barry interjected. I couldn't see but I knew he had that characteristic sly grin on his face as he said it.

"I guess I just needed Tess to…"

"Be there for you," Barry finished.

"Yes, that. But I just feel like she's been totally oblivious to what's been going on…and it's not because I haven't told her…or at least tried to. Then, to add to that, she's going through something—what exactly I don't know—and the only reason I know that much is because Giara has been dropping hints again but you know how vague those are and I…"

"Warren, just keep focusing on pitching yourself as the go-to guy. You've got a week 'til they make a decision. Worry about everything else later."

"Yeah," I said robotically agreeing with him at the sound of a brief pause. He continued on but by then, I was half listening. Once again entranced by the city, I began thinking about Tess and me, trying to figure out how I could be so out of the loop about what's going on with her, and she with me.

"Warren? Where'd you go, man?" Barry asked after realizing I'd zoned out on him.

"Sorry. Just thinking," I said.

"So are you staying the night or…"

"I really should be going home to my wife tonight," I said.

"I know, I know. And I should be out buying Jackie two-dozen white roses and begging at her window for forgiveness. I did stand her up tonight to be with *you* during *your* time of crisis, you know," he paused, sighing heavily. "But I'm here. Come to bed. We'll both make amends to our women tomorrow."

"I think I'm just going to head home," I replied. I wanted to stay…I felt at ease with Barry…but I didn't want to have to concoct another story about some deal and a deadline and sleeping on the sofa at the office again. Tess had been naïve enough to believe that at least half a dozen times before and each time it killed me because I knew she didn't deserve to be lied to. I also knew that had I told her the truth about where I had been it would've hurt her more. *I can't lie to her again, not with everything going on.* "Thanks for the chat Barry," I said picking up my coat and keys.

"Suit yourself. Lock up will you? I don't feel like getting up."

"Sure, I've got my key," I said blowing out the last two candles that had yet to burn out.

The taste of a drop of blood trickling into my mouth snapped me out of my flashback. I reached for some tissue to wipe the drops of blood from my face. As I did, I realized that I didn't even remember driving home—not getting on I-85, not paying the toll on GA 400, nothing. *How dangerous is that? It's like I'm a living zombie.* I finished drying my face then headed down the hallway back to the bedroom. I stripped down to my boxers and climbed into bed, my mind still trying to figure it all out. *I can't go on like this. I've got to...*

"Baby, you're frowning," Tess said, breaking into my thoughts. I hadn't even heard her come in. "What's wrong?" she asked sliding under the covers and wrapping her arms around me. "Something happen at work?"

If I had had the strength, I would have told her everything that was on my mind but I didn't. Instead, I just pulled her close to me and kissed her on the forehead. "Don't worry about it Tess. I'm fine. Everything is fine."

## *Analysis*

Oh, what a tangled web we weave when we try to paint the picture that society has laid out for us—instead of what's real. This story appears at first to reflect the lives of people who are financially well-off and should be living what we call "the good life". However, the emotional detachment of the characters has created a scenario so distorted from the original picture that it leaves one to wonder what happened here.

Well it's simple. People will try to get their needs met any way possible. Initially when most of us set out to create our adult life, we embark with a lot of ideals, practices and concepts placed in us by others. We continue to hope that our efforts will render us the magnificent results that we have heard about, that we believe other people may have achieved through similar efforts.

Our first goal is to make money, buy stuff, acquire beautiful surroundings and people, and look like we have it going on. The people who focus on attaining this definition of success will often find the fruits of their labors to *be* successful, and then upon achieving that success, they find themselves wondering what it was that they initially were trying to achieve. They begin to figure out that they have confused what they really wanted with what they were *told* they should want. "I want a beautiful wife that makes me look good"; then what he ends up with is a superficial woman who at all costs must look good and must have the best with no regards to the needs of others. He may end up with a woman that is not interested in his troubles or what he has to go through to get her the things that she desires.

But his desire for her was based in a selfish ego and what he attracted was a selfish, ego-driven woman. Remember we draw to us people and circumstances that reflect where we are. When our goal is for one thing, we often tune our senses out to the other things because they are not important to us at the time; and when they become important, it is too late to change the order of priority or decide that you want it to be something else. If I go to buy a television and I say I want it to come with Picture-in-Picture, but I don't *buy* one with PiP, then it for sure will not have PiP when I get that TV home. If it does not come with what it is that you desire, trust and believe it won't be there when you desire it.

The first thing here is that you have to realize that success is not determined by others but by you. Success should not be motivated by fear of lack, or by some insecure need to prove something to another. Now, I'm not saying that actions motivated by these factors won't drive a person to produce desired results, but I am saying that if these factors are the motivation for success, then when you *do* achieve the success there will be a void of some sort upon arrival at that destination.

You see, we are self-sustaining beings. To truly achieve a fulfilling success, we must turn within and follow our inner guide to lead us independently of the opinions of others to where it is that we will find success specifically designed for us personally. Warren, by his own behaviors, has trained/allowed his family to expect and act a certain way, and then expects them to act differently when the situation is different. Sorry, that will never work. What you put in you get out. You will never squeeze an orange and get apple juice. Warren has painted this picture of himself handling everything and not wanting the input or compassion of his family because *he is the man*, and he can handle it all. It is going to be okay because Daddy's *got it covered*. His family has been conditioned to operate in this fashion, but now Warren needs something different from them and does not know what to do.

As I said before, the intention of humans is to get their needs met. So if Warren is unable to get his intimacy needs met at home, he finds other ways. As spiritual beings we seek unity and connection and are drawn to each other's energy, as we are all of, and a part of, the same source. We are like water; we seek our own level. Well, our desire is intimacy, a connection to one another, a sense of returning home. We are spiritual beings in human bodies. Our bodies do have genders, but our souls are androgynous. Therefore, spiritual intimacy can be achieved regardless of ego gender. This may be confusing to someone who has not taken the time to understand this blueprint. If intimacy is what I desire and I am able to achieve it with a being of the same gender, then the goal is achieved. Warren gets his intimacy needs met with his relationship with Barry in a way he is unable to achieve with Tess, despite the fact that he loves her and is attracted to her.

Society plays a huge role in our challenges in developing healthy, happy relationships. Women are socialized to be caring, nurturing, vulnerable and emotional, and they are praised and rewarded for these qualities. Men, who have the same desires as women (because after all, we are all spiritual beings), are socialized with an aversion to having certain emotions, to being nurturing, to showing their feelings, and to being vulnerable. If you are a male and you have these feelings, you are taught that you must shut them down in order to be accepted. Then what you find yourself left with is two beings—man and woman—who have the same core desire but with two different approaches to achieving it, without a bridge by which the two can join together successfully.

Now, I'm not saying the two never meet, but it has proven to be amazingly difficult to merge these different male and female styles. It requires a lot of retraining and determination for the relationship to be successful. It's as though the man is on the low road and the woman is on the high road, emotionally speaking, and that the goal of intimacy is in the middle, but we are expected to arrive at the same destination. I am physically attracted to you, but everything about your actions puts me off, and the aggravation it takes just to achieve minimal moments of successful intimacy with you is just not always worth it. Male and female become like oil and vinegar. They taste good together but they never blend.

Then, when you get around someone who has been gender-socialized the same as you have and you are able to relax, be yourself, and find the peace and intimacy that you seek, you find yourself strangely attracted and wanting to experience it in what you believe to be the fullness of it. Some people mistakenly think that the way to achieve that "full experience" involves sex. You have longed for the peace that this intimacy brings and you don't care what package it's in. You just don't want to have to explain it to the world.

We are taught that because sex feels good and that we are told that it *is* intimacy that it logically follows that it should be the next step whenever we feel attracted or intimate and close to someone. Unfortunately, this is not true and this erroneous belief sometimes takes people down paths of perversion and confusion. Sometimes it even creates an environment for heterosexual individuals to engage in behavior not in line with their natural sexual persuasion. This applies to women as well as men. Even though this behavior feels wrong, the overwhelming desire for intimacy in an environment where you feel understood and related to seems to prevail. Of course, this does not happen with and to everyone. We are all on different journeys but in today's society, it appears to be happening a lot more often.

This situation would be resolved if we would stop looking for the quick fix and buying into what feels good for the moment. Sometimes you have to say no to good to say yes to great. If you find that the behaviors in which you have been engaging are not rendering you the results you desire, you may want to try a new way. Stop and take a look at your situation. Ask yourself what it is that you are trying to accomplish. Then ask why you desire what it is you desire. Figure out if the desire is motivated by love or fear. Fear-based motivation should be examined to determine why the fear exists. When you determine the fear, replace it with the truth and remind yourself of that truth continuously until it becomes second nature.

Sounds too simple? Try it first before you knock it. It really works. Here is an example to help you with this practice. "Women don't understand me and constantly nag at me." So, you find yourself in situations where you are constantly bickering with your partner. But the truth is that you have communications problems, because you are afraid to expose yourself to your partner for fear that she will think that you are weak, inferior or not strong enough to handle certain things. So you suffer in silence, frustrated and resentful that you can't express your feelings. This makes you feel lonely and like you have to protect yourself from the people that you perceive are waiting for the opportunity to criticize you when in actuality, the people that you are around probably would love to be a part of your inner world and are waiting for an opportunity to support you and create with you.

For women, a good example of this is the belief that there are not enough good single men to go around. Some women find themselves dating married men or men with girlfriends. In fact the underlying factor to this is that if you thought that you were worthy of having a good man all to yourself, you would not allow unavailable men to invade your space. Ask yourself: if you were everything that you thought you should be, would you have a difficult time securing your own exclusive man? Does your answer match your current belief? Probably not...so then ask yourself what changed? The only thing that changed was your opinion and standard of and for yourself.

Realize that you create your existence and the easy way out is not always the *best* way out. Sometimes you have to make the decisions that seem to be the most difficult, but the results are so much more rewarding. Benjamin Franklin once said that "...the definition of insanity is doing the same thing over and over and expecting different results". Is this what *you* do? If you find that what you've been doing isn't giving you the results you really want, maybe its time to find and develop different practices and not just create different dilemmas.

# 4.   *Game Recognizes Game*

*Get it together, Alex. Look at yourself. Your pits are sweating, your cheeks are flushed and damn it if you didn't let that man get so close you started getting wet. This is not you.* I was staring into the mirror in the bathroom at the back of the cabana. I could hear the music from the party booming, the bass shaking the air freshener on top of the toilet. Still, the thoughts running through my mind were louder. *Don't let some cocky, wannabe ladies' man get to you. How could you have let it get this far? This isn't how the plan was supposed to go. Got to regroup. Think, girl. How are you going to get yourself out of this one?*

I don't know why but every since I was a teenager, I've enjoyed breaking men down who were too full of themselves, especially the pretty ones. I guess that's why I was so drawn to Anthony. I had heard of him before. After all, he was an A-list celebrity…in the Black community, at least…but for whatever reason, I had never paid him much attention until about a week ago.

Monday:

I was doing my daily bedtime workout when a voice on the TV caught my attention. It was a deep baritone voice, but despite its sex appeal, it wasn't the voice itself that made me pause mid-stride from my bicycle crunches. It was what the voice said. I looked up to see Anthony Johns chatting with Letterman. I suppose they had been talking about the usual—

his new movie and the lack of him having a date at the Oscars® this year—but it wasn't until Letterman asked Anthony what it would take for a woman to make him retire from chronic bachelordom that my ears perked up.

As Anthony started to give his answer, the camera caught him on an extreme close-up, his light green eyes looking directly into the camera. It was as if he was speaking to me directly. Without batting an eye, breaking a smirk or even altering his pitch he confidently proclaimed: "It'll never happen. I just don't think my perfect package exists. I'd even venture to say that there is no single woman cunning enough to keep me satisfied, not for a lifetime." Sitting up, I looked directly into the screen, watching as Anthony and Letterman cackled like hyenas over the comment. *That's one conceited Mo' Fo. He needs to know cocky is not cute.* Right then and there, I knew that he was going to be my next conquest.

Tuesday:

I went into stealth mode. I started working the phones while having lunch at the Hard Rock Cafe. With the palm trees blowing and the invigorating scent of the Biscayne Bay tickling my senses, it was my favorite planning spot. Sipping the last bit of my Mimosa, I finally reached a friend who has a friend who knew Anthony. I turned on the charm and boy, did he come through. Turned out my timing couldn't have been more perfect. The friend of my friend, Char, was having a get together at her place and he, my friend BJ, was able to score invitations for both of us. *Chance meeting, orchestrated.*

Next, I began doing my research. "You can't win a battle if you don't know your enemy." That's what my dad always taught me. I hopped on the net like any other self-respecting makeshift sleuth, and I Googled Anthony. I found all sorts of information—about his childhood, his favorite this and that, the scandals he'd been involved in, and the jackpot: a compilation of all of the women he had coupled with over the last eight years. I stayed up all night sorting through the information and taking note of all the things I thought would be helpful. By 3 am Thursday morning, I knew his turn-ons, turn-offs, and how he usually dealt with women: Those he's not interested in seriously he beds and flaunts at this event or that; then she disappears. When he's interested in a woman though, he basically treats her like he could care less about much of anything she says or does. *Typical man!* I also had a good idea of the type of women he had been attracted to in the past and the woman I would become to bait him into making me the next.

Thursday:

There was no particular look Anthony went for, at least not from what I could tell. He had dated women with weaves down their backs, women who had short afros, women with locks and twists, women with relaxed hair, blondes, brunettes, black women, white women, Asian women, Hispanics, Scandinavians…the list went on and on, so I knew from jump that my physical appearance wasn't the main draw for him. Physically, he seemed to just like women who were stacked: breasts, butt, hips and toned legs but I had all that covered. I did notice that they all seemed to be natural beauties, little or no make-up and that they all had a low-key sexiness about them. They were intelligent women too, all of them independently making money and well into their careers. I also studied the stories surrounding the various break-ups with the women Anthony had dated. Based on that, I created a profile of the type of woman he likes: she is outspoken but not boisterous, sexy but unaware of her full appeal, stylish but not a label whore, and she is both smart and witty.

As I walked through the mall, I continued designing this woman in my mind. How she speaks, walks, dresses, even the facial expressions she makes; it all played like an old 1960's-style how-to video in my head. I passed up my usual haunts like BCBG and White House Black Market and headed for the department store instead. After all, I was there to find something Anthony would like, not what I liked.

Scouring the racks, I tried to find natural fabrics that had tailored, clean lines to them. The outfit I needed had to have a hint of sexy but leave a whole lot to the imagination and it had to have that "effortlessly put together" look about it. I tried on outfits for two hours but finally settled on a drape neck Mango-print blouse that dipped down to the navel and a white, bias cut, calf-length linen skirt. *Airy enough for an outdoor party on a sunny Miami day; implies cleavage without showing any breasts; a subtle hint of innocence. Game on.*

Friday:

I found out through Donna and Ilana Michaels, a.k.a. the queens of the black elite, a.k.a. the most infamous gossip terrors in Miami, that Anthony was going to be at Bed, a sexy South Beach spot. So, I called my girls Caprice and Micah and let them know we were going clubbing. I went for a manicure and pedicure during lunch and snuck away from work an hour early to get an emergency facial. I figured that if I was going for the natural beauty look, I needed to look as naturally vibrant as I could.

We went to Bed around midnight. The club was packed with the locals who wanted to front like they had something going on, B-list celebrities who were trying to network so they could get something going on, and a nice brood of household name A-list celebrities and socialites who actually *did* have it going on. I hadn't anticipated having to dress for a club so I had to go shopping in my own closet to piece together an outfit suitable for the club and Anthony's tastes. I had decided on a tailored pedal pusher suit—white, of course—with a strapless, blush pink pinstriped camisole underneath and my white, strappy, stiletto Manolo sandals to set off the American Pedicure I'd had done earlier that day. I clipped my hair up into a flirty ponytail and forewent my usual eye shadow, blush, and Peach Dream lipstick, opting for a thin coat of brown eyeliner and a lip gloss that was a shade darker than my natural lip color.

I began scanning the club as soon as I walked through the front door. The plan was to make myself the center of attention, taking the spotlight off Anthony. I wanted to do it right after he made his big entrance, limiting his time in the limelight. I knew that it would intrigue him that someone, an unknown at that, could take attention away from "America's Hunkiest Heartthrob Anthony Johns". So, I looked around the club to find a dance partner. I needed someone who had had one too many drinks and didn't care about anything but having fun. I spotted a tall, muscular man with short, shiny black hair, blue eyes and golden skin: an Italian Adonis. One thing I had learned living in Miami is that people are never who you think they are, let alone speak the language you would expect. I used the universal language to let him know I wanted to dance with him: body language. I walked up behind him, pressed my breasts up against his back, circled around him halfway, then started dancing in front of him. He smiled then grabbed my hand as he led me out onto the dance floor.

It took Anthony forever to arrive and I ended up out on the dance floor with my Adonis longer than I had anticipated. My feet were throbbing and I was on the brink of going from moist to sweaty. But just as I was about to take a break, the music shut off and women started screaming. I knew Anthony had walked in. Just as the DJ was undoubtedly about to announce that Anthony was in the house I screamed out, "Mr. DJ…That was my song. Can't you see I'm trying to groove!" I knew that tonight's DJ was infamous for putting people on the spot, trying to make them look silly. He didn't disappoint that night either.

"All right then," he said, pulling out a record from his stash. "Since you just *have* to dance, this one's just for you. Let me see what you got."

Sean Paul started blasting from the speakers. I grabbed on to my Adonis, closed my eyes and went to work. Caprice and Micah joined me on the dance floor, dragging a couple guys with them and we set the club off. I watched as Anthony and his entourage walked towards the VIP. From the corner of my eye, I could see that his boys were watching me but he wasn't, so I took it up a notch. The DJ called out, "Watch out now!" and Anthony's attention turned back towards the dance floor. I turned my back to him and focused on my Adonis during the bridge of the song then turned back around to face Anthony. I caught his gaze and kept it, moving as if I were dancing with him. His lips parted into a smile and he cocked his head to the side, motioning for me to come up to the VIP with him. *Tempting. Could be fun to improvise instead of sticking to my plan.* I smiled back and shook my head slowly from side to side. *But I don't think so. I'm not the hit and quit it for the night. Got longer term plans for us.* As the song was ending, I gave a smile and wink in Anthony's direction then turned back around, hugged my Adonis and started grooving to the next song. I watched as the VIP filled up with groupies. Anthony poked his head out above the sea of silicone cleavage and mini skirts. I ducked behind my Adonis' shoulder to watch without being seen. *Looking for me, huh? Good.* Pleased with myself, I snuck off the dance floor, said my goodbyes to my friends then headed home. *Bet I know who you'll be dreamin' about tonight…no matter who's in the bed with you. And tomorrow, you'll meet your dream girl.*

Saturday:

I got dressed in the outfit I bought earlier in the week and headed over to Char Pincinni's. BJ was meeting me there. As I walked through the house and out towards the back lawn where most of the festivities were taking place, I noticed a live Calypso band was playing inside the Great Hall of the mansion, and fashionably dressed, unnaturally beautiful people were strategically posted throughout the estate, motionlessly posed. *Fashion line launch party.* I headed down the Grecian stone staircase past the Olympic-size walk-in pool to the bar to get a glass of Moscato.

The plan today was to not only get Anthony's attention but to hold it and make him want me. But I knew that I had to do it in a way that he felt like *he* was controlling things and that whatever I did had to stand out from the high-priced hoochies that were bound to be throwing themselves at him. I also knew that I only had one shot at meeting him face to face so staying close to Char until Anthony and I had been introduced was a must.

As I was returning to the house from the bar, I saw BJ waving at me from the top of the stairs. I watched as the six-foot three, 235 lb man bounded down the steps, smiling wider then the Cheshire cat and wearing a plaid baby blue and brown linen shirt complete with matching cropped pants and brown Birkenstocks. *Bless his heart. He tried.* I pointed towards the house. He nodded, realizing that I wanted to go back inside. Char was in there mingling with guests as they arrived and I wanted to be sure to be close when Anthony got there.

I didn't have to wait long. Anthony strolled in looking every bit as debonair as I knew he thought he was—watch blinging out of control, hair glistening, pecs peeking out of his shirt, and dark tinted sunglasses. He spotted Char and headed in her direction. I grabbed BJ's arm and started making my way in Anthony's direction. I figured that I'd intercept him just before he reached Char. *They'll both have to acknowledge me that way.* I stepped in his path then stopped to wave at a nonexistent person outside. He paused and I could feel his eyes studying me, indignant that someone had gotten in his way. Lowering his sunglasses slightly, he took a closer look.

"Don't I know you? "He asked, tilting his head to the side.

"No," I responded dryly. *He's cuter close up than I thought he would be.*

"I'm sure I do," he rebutted, sliding his glasses back in place.

"I'm sure you'd just like to," I said trying to sound standoffish and slipping my pink tinted sunglasses on and glancing around the room. *I can go tit for tat with you. If you want to be mysterious, so can I.*

"BJ, it's obvious your friend isn't shy," Char said, pausing briefly and looking me over from head to toe. "What's her name?"

BJ cleared his throat then bowed forward as if addressing royalty, "Madame Char this is Alexus Carpenter. Alex, meet Char Pincinni. And," he began standing up and facing Anthony, "I am…"

"Anthony Johns, this is my good friend BJ Parker and my new friend Alexus Carpenter," Char chimed in.

"Alex," I corrected her.

"Right. Alex Carpenter," she repeated.

"I know. I saw you in Bed last night," Anthony said.

*He definitely was paying attention. That's good. If he had just been sizing me up for a one-night stand, he probably wouldn't even have remembered me.* "Sorry, I slept alone last night," I replied with a flirty smile.

"I mean you were at Bed, dancing with some guy in the center of the floor. You had on a sexy white suit and…"

"You got me. I was there," I said smiling, moving in closer and looking up at him, "but I don't remember seeing you there."

"Oh, you got jokes. You looked right at me when you were on the dance floor."

"You must be mistaken. I look at the whole crowd when I'm dancing but really, it's all just one big blur. But listen, we can sort all this out later. I see someone I must chat with," I said, nodding a cordial goodbye to Char then grabbing BJ's arm gently and heading towards the front door. *And Alex takes the lead.*

I spent the next hour mingling with folks I could care less about and keeping within Anthony's line of sight. I knew that he was not the type of man who liked being left and that eventually, he would approach me again to finish the conversation we had started. *Be patient Alex. He's got to feel like he's the one in control. And remember, play it innocent, let him do all the talking so you can get the information you need to plan the next play.*

Four hours. I waited nearly the entire party for him and he still hadn't come over to me so I seized an opportunity when he stopped by the carving stations to get a plate of shaved barbecue beef. Though I was pissed at the wait, I knew it was a good sign. It meant he liked me.

"An actor who's not a Vegan? Well aren't you the rare find," I said peeking around his shoulder at his plate.

"I am. But that has nothing to do with what I eat," he said drenching his beef with more sauce.

*What an egotistical jerk. Wait. Did he just flirt back? That's not how he operates. Maybe he doesn't...*

"So are you done mingling with all your big time friends, you know, to chat with little 'ol me?"

*Bait taken. Do your thang, Alex.*

"If so, we could go down by Char's cabana. Should be a bit more intimate down there," he continued, popping some of the beef into his mouth and licking his fingers.

*Alone time? So soon? That's different. I thought he usually held out until the woman desperately makes the first move, whether he likes them or not.*

I had the chef fix me a barbecue beef sandwich. Then, we headed down the path towards the cabana. The conversation was fairly generic, just talking about whom we'd met at the party and hashing out how he knew Char and I knew BJ. Right before we went into the cabin, Anthony turned and smiled at me, slyly. I couldn't read what was on his mind but I could guess. *No. No. No. I thought we'd already established I'm not the booty call. Man! If this cat thinks he's getting in my panties just 'cause he's fine with those piercing eyes and thick, juicy lips he's so off point.*

He stared at me for a moment then leaned in. I closed my eyes, bracing for a kiss but felt the slight touch of his lips on the corner of my mouth. Chills spread from the corner of my lips through every inch of my body. *Was that supposed to be sexy? A corner of the mouth kiss? Come on, this guy has to have better game than this. If this is all he's got, he's going to disappoint with the quickness.* He pulled back from me, licking his lips.

"Next time, try to get all the barbecue sauce in your mouth and I won't have to do that," he said turning his back and walking into the cabana.

"You could've just told me it was there," I said wiping my lips with a napkin. *That wasn't game. That was flirting—blatant, kind of sweet flirting—but from what I read, that's not his usual move. He usually...*

"Yes, I could've," he responded.

*He flirted again. Why's he doing that? New game? Ignore it. You're in control Alex. Make him play your game.*

"So what movies have you been in again," I asked. He looked at me, scanning my face to see if I was about to crack a smile as if I were playing a joke on him. I looked back at him, concentrating on maintaining my best "no really, I'm clueless" face. He laughed to himself then began reeling off the movies he'd starred in.

"Wow. That was you? You look so...different in person," I replied.

He grabbed me and pulled me close to him, reciting a line from the movie he'd won an Image Award for earlier that year. With my body pressed against his, I could feel his muscles tense beneath his clothing. *Wasn't expecting that one. Nice build. Definitely wasn't a body double in his last flick. Oh God, he's wearing Marc Jacobs. I love Marc Jacobs cologne.*

"Do I?" he asked still holding me.

"Yes. You do," I said pushing him away and checking out the rest of the cabana. *He's already interjected contact twice. That's pretty quick. I always wait until I've got them lost in thoughts about themselves before I surprise 'em with something like that.*

I had to give him points for that move. He'd caught me off guard. Usually by that point, I'd have found some fatal flaw in the guy to focus on so even if something like that happened, it didn't affect me. Some guys looked good but had horrid breath, or when they spoke a wad of spittle gathered in the corner of their mouth, or they mispronounced words, had lip sweat, etc.—something to make it easy to play the game without getting caught up in what they were saying or doing. But this guy, he didn't have any of that. *All right. Let's see if he can keep up his game if I keep eye contact. He'll break after a few minutes. Men can't handle that. Too easy to read them.*

I stood across from him, listening to what he was saying. As he moved about the room, I tracked him, maintaining eye contact. Then he stopped, sat down on the edge of the sofa and stared at me. He didn't say anything for what seemed like an eternity. I could feel his eyes penetrating me, like they were searching for something. I've never been the type one would call an "open book" but at that moment, I felt he was reading me like one. I didn't know how to react because though I wanted to turn away, it was as if his eyes were telling his story too. That cold, cockiness I'd seen in his eyes that night he was on the Letterman show was gone and for a moment, he looked different to me somehow. *What is that? I know men's looks but that one was different.* I could feel myself begin to fidget, feeling for something, anything of interest on the table to turn my attention to.

"You strike me as the type of woman who much prefers to be heard rather than do all the listening. Besides, I bet you know more about me than you're letting on. So who is Alexus Carpenter?" he asked, finally breaking the silence.

"Alex," I corrected. "I'm a buyer for an auction house who likes to cut loose on the dance floor on occasion. Plain and simple."

"You know, with all that music outside, I really can't hear you that well. Why don't you come and sit over here," he said, pointing to a leather chair about five feet from the loveseat arm he was perched on.

*If we're going to get closer, you're the one that's going to have to do the moving.*

"I didn't ask what you did Alexus. I asked who you are," he pushed.

"It's Alex."

"Well I prefer Alexus. What's a beautiful woman like you doing calling herself by such a masculine name anyway? Are you hiding from something? Is your name a way to put up your tough exterior…"

"It's just a nickname," I began.

"…or is it another persona you slip on when you need to," he continued. I stared at him for a moment, figuring out his game plan. *He wants me on the defensive. He thinks that if he gets to me, I'll be vulnerable and he'll be able to take control. I invented that play. Amateur. Let's see how you react to it.*

"Only the weak find it necessary to live their lives playing roles. By the way, are you playing a scene from one of your movies now or is this the real you? Never can tell with you actor types."

"Actors play off of one another. There's no scene if there's not another actor to play to. So, you tell me," he said sliding down into the loveseat, one leg still hanging over the side.

*He's better at this than I thought. The indirect route isn't going to work to bait this guy. Let's see how he does if I go right at him.*

"Anthony,…"

"Yes, Alexus?"

*Why does he keep calling me that? Is he dumb or just disrespectful?*

"…why did you drag me back here? What do you want? Some tail? 'Cause I'm not the one. There's plenty of hoo…"

"I didn't drag you back here. You're here because you want to be here, as am I. We would have ended up back here together, or some other place in the house, eventually. I'm sure of it. There's just something about you that I…"

"Well I don't know how you can be sure of it. I didn't even know you before today," I replied.

"Yes, you did."

"No. I didn't."

"I know when a woman has her sights set on me. The chicks lookin' for a baby daddy. I can spot 'em a mile away. Gold diggers, they have a stench about them called desperation. The ones who want to ride the coattails of my fame, I can see through their act right away. Fix me a Hennessey, no ice."

I moved over to the bar and began fixing his drink, pissed that he was even putting me in the same category as those women. "So what do you think? That I'm some groupie? I don't need you, your money, your…," I barked back, handing him his drink. *What the hell did I just do?*

"You, I haven't figured out what it is you want. I haven't locked on to your scent…yet."

"I don't want anything from you," I said, trying to sound annoyed.

"Yes, you do," he pushed. "Everyone wants something."

"Okay, fine. I want a fabulous career but that has absolutely nothing to do with you unless you're planning on getting into the auction house business."

"And?"

"And that's it," I said shrugging my shoulders.

"I think you want more than that. You want sex. You want love. You want intimacy," he started. "Don't be embarrassed. The attraction is mutual."

"Wow. I am not attrac...What? Are you practicing for a new role or something? If so, keep at it because playing head doc is not working for you. And be sure to stick to the script," I said sarcastically.

"Right. And I bet you even want to not be the one who's always in control. Like right now," he paused, raising his eyebrow, a crooked smile forming on his lips.

*This guy is too full of himself!*

"I bet if I came over there, grabbed you up into my arms and kissed your neck," he said getting up and walking over to me, "say here, then here, and here," he whispered, touching me behind my ear, on the side of my neck and then on my right shoulder blade, "you'd go weak in my arms in one second flat." *Those are my spots. Please don't do it. Please. I will have you laid out on this floor and ride you like one of Char's prize stallions.*

"This is not *Gone With the Wind* and you certainly are not Rhett Butler," I said busting out in laughter.

"Maybe not but it's true," he said turning around abruptly and sitting back down. "You don't have the stamina to withstand me."

"Now you're the one who's got jokes," I said, plopping down on the loveseat next to him. *That's right, Alex. Call his bluff. Show him you can get as close as you want.* "I'm quite certain, Mr. Johns," I whispered, leaning in close to him. "I have enough stamina to keep you smiling for days on end." *No man's going to tell me what I can and can't handle.*

"You think so? Then kiss me, just a peck on the lips, and see how well your stamina is then," he challenged.

I looked into his eyes, searching for some hint of where he was going with all this. Nothing. "Why would I want to kiss you? I'm not even attracted to you."

"Yes, you are Alexus but you won't admit that. It's not your style. And I know it's not because you don't want to admit it. It's because you don't want to want to."

*Damn. What did I just do that he could have caught that? Think Alex., What signs are you giving that you're not supposed to.* As I was trying to figure things out, he moved in closer, touching my thigh. I felt my lips quiver, the ones hidden beneath my thong. *What the hell was that?* Trying to hold my composure, I stood up, letting his hand fall to the sofa, and asked him where the bathroom was located. He smiled to himself then pointed behind him. *Cocky bastard.*

I strolled off slowly until I was out of Anthony's line of sight then scurried the rest of the way to the bathroom. I dropped my purse on the floor and grabbed some tissue to dab the sweat away that was forming on my top lip. *Get it together, Alex. Look at yourself. Your pits are sweating, your cheeks are flushed and damn it if you didn't let that man get so close that you started getting wet. This is not you. Don't let some cocky, wannabe ladies' man, fine and charming as he may be, get to you. How could you have let it get this far? This isn't how the plan was supposed to go. Got to regroup. Think, girl. How are you going to get yourself out of this one?*

I stared into the mirror running through everything that had just happened. *He's not going to win. He is not. How am I going to turn the tables on him? Okay, I can't stay here. Too tempting to…the wine and the heat must be getting to me, making me let my guard down so he can get in those cheap shots, but I'm running this game. He's got too much advantage here. That's it. I got to get him back out with the rest of the party. All those near-naked chicks should help to throw him off his game and then I can…*

"Alexus. You okay?" I heard Anthony shout from the living room.

I touched up my eyeliner and gloss then headed back out to the living room. "Aren't you the anxious one? Having flash-backs of all the women who ran out on you?"

"There you go with the jokes again. I like that though," he replied. "You make me laugh. Come do your routine right here and make me laugh some more," he said patting the seat cushion next to him.

"I would, but you see," I said picking up my wine glass, "my Moscato is warm and if I sit there, there won't be any smartly dressed waiters hustling over to me to exchange it for a fresh glass…unless you're willing to be my errand boy."

"Alexus, come sit down," he said patting the sofa once again.

I felt my legs start to move in his direction. Part of me wanted stay and see what would happen if I went and sat down next to him. *You don't obey anyone. You're running this game, Alex, not him. He's the one that does what you want, not the other way around.* Will took over and I turned towards the cabana door. "Don't think so," I said stopping in front of the sliding door. I waited for a few moments, my back still to Anthony. "Anthony, the door please. We need fresh drinks." I slanted my eyes left, looking out the corner of my eye to see if he was responding. Shaking his head and smiling to himself, he got up. He slid the door open slightly wider than the width of his body and stepped through, partially. *Forced body-to-body contact is your best play right now? You got nothing.*

"You're something else, aren't you," he asked.

"Yes, I am," I said, squeezing past him. *Round one goes to the lovely Alex.*

## *Analysis*

We have heard that life is a game, but that is a false statement. Games require strategy and manipulation of yourself and others. There are calculations involved and the need for planned results to be successful.

This sounds a little like life, but the difference is that the planning or design of life was already done before you opened your eyes to life, and if you apply the "game-playing" plan for your life, you would be setting yourself up for a discontented existence. Life only resembles a game, but it can not be *played* or you will find yourself *being* played.

To lead a successful life, you must allow life to happen through you by appreciating every experience that you encounter. The real power is in your release and submission to your journey. It is there that you are able to have life and experience it more abundantly. Isn't it funny that we feel more comfortable interacting with people when we think that we are controlling their reactions to us and their actions with us? But the truth of the matter is that because of our own insecurities and inability to trust the process of life, we allow our fears to devise plans to try and get what we believe to be the best situation and results for ourselves. In actuality, because our knowledge of our existence is veiled and our vision is tunneled, we are not even aware of how great things can be. So what happens is that we limit our results by attempting to control them. Ironic, isn't it? Not believing that the universe has your best interest in mind and that by just being alive you automatically deserve the best that life has to offer, we get in the way of our own effortless achievement.

Alexus has really just been doing way too much. She looks confident and is highly intelligent, maybe a little too intelligent for her own good; she hides behind these characteristics, and that usually gets her the kudos of others. In fact, she really believes that she has to earn the things she has and the people she attracts. She believes that she has to prove herself worthy through her actions to receive the things that she desires. Nothing could be further from the truth. In her schemes, she has to deny herself the feelings that she so longs to express because she feels that allowing her spirit to express itself in truth would get in the way of her ego's plans.

From the time we are born, we are socialized out of being who we truly are into what others desire us to be. In this process, we develop compensatory skills to cope with the duality of existence that is being instilled in us. These behavioral patterns become the armor that we adorn ourselves with and sport through life.

The sad truth here is that you don't need armor: it is an unnecessary weight that we carry around. It is our baggage. We don't need armor because we don't need protection. Our Creator is the only protector that we need. Source knows all, sees all, and is capable of doing all. Why would you need anything else? And on top of that, you are the loving heir of the Creator and you are God's greatest concern. We start to take things into our own hands because we are taught to believe that we are our Egos instead of our Essence.

So the simplest solution would be to start identifying with who you truly are...the spirit within. The reason that you are able to have everlasting life is because you are *not* the body that you dwell within. The body is just a host, a vehicle if you will, that affords you the ability to express yourself in the physical realm; a realm that provides the opportunity for a spiritual being to have life more abundantly.

Sometimes we get so caught up in what we are doing that we don't see what has already been done. We have to keep in mind that our souls are drawn to each other to assist themselves in the expression and experiences of this plain. The people that we like and the ones that we despise are all apart of our spiritual expression. Without their participation, we would be unable to be aware of the things that life has to reveal to us. Most of the adverse situations in which we find ourselves are there because of our denial of who we are, what we feel, and what we were designed to do. If we allow ourselves the joy of expressing what we feel, what we think, and what we want to do, we will find that life becomes sweet. We will see that our true intentions, exempt from fear, are nothing but pure goodness.

Allow yourself to spend time reprogramming your thoughts and actions. Ask yourself what it is that you *really* want without caring what the world has told you that you *should* want. Allow yourself to express what it is you really feel without consideration of how it will make you look to others or what others could do to you if they knew how you felt. At first, you will find this process difficult, but know that that is just withdrawal from bad habits. Forge through that discomfort. The prize at the end of this process is so great! So trust me—it will be well worth it. After all, living life the way you currently do is quite laborious and tumultuous and at the end there is still no prize for winning "the game", because there *is* no game! Doing it this way may be tumultuous, but there is a huge reward of peace, happiness and self-expression. This method of living gives you self-awareness and when you know how great you are, the power of this awareness is limitless.

Life is designed to equip you with what you need to experience the light within. Games have a "point system" and reward people based on ability. Life has natural consequences that are determined by your understanding and your ability to implement what you understand. It is not a game, but a natural unfolding or awakening to the magnificence of your spirituality, your greatness. There is no need for you to play games with your life because you can create whatever it is that you desire by just understanding what it is you want and preparing yourself to receive it. Your thoughts create your desires and your actions create the expression in the form of what you want. I read a bumper sticker once that said, "Thoughts become things, so pick the good ones". I know this to be excellent advice, and this is something of which you would want to constantly remind yourself, because we are constantly thinking.

When you play games with your life, you find that because of your limited vision and awareness you create limited results that are not always as satisfying as you would like. So know that what you don't know can't hurt you, but it surely can limit you.

It might appear to be fun being the host in the game of life; but by not allowing yourself to experience all that life has to offer because you are so busy controlling the expression of how and what you think you want it to be, you cheat yourself out of the expression and fullness that is there already. Games have too many restrictions and guidelines; true life flows uninhibited. What we have to realize is that desire is of God, and if you have a desire, it is a part of the journey necessary for you to arrive at your ultimate destination, so count it all good. But if you are able to get a level of understanding as to how this thing we call life goes, the knowledge will elevate you to higher awareness and expose you to greater joy.

So, here is some food for thought for those that are interested. Whenever you desire something, go within and begin to prepare yourself for it and know that when you are ready it will come. It's like when you know you are going to an exclusive party. You start preparing before the appointed time. You get yourself ready and when the time arrives, you go. The same process needs to happen in your daily life. Decide what you want to do and prepare yourself for that. Then go forth to receive it with a confidence that you are expected there and everything that you desire will be present.

This retraining does require discipline and vulnerability, but tricks are for kids and when you become adults you need to put away childish ways. Life is short and can be amazingly effortless when the right system is applied. Fun does not have to be a temporary state. Dr Wayne Dyer says that there is no "way" to happiness; happiness *is* the way. This little phrase has a powerful impact. Just become what it is that you desire for your life and then you will have what it is that you desire in your life. No need to run from what you don't want in an effort to achieve what it is that you think that you want. Just identify what you want, allow yourself to be that thing for yourself, and be liberated in the expression of that without considering the negative energy of others. Then watch how the complexion and expression of your life will change. Awareness changes perception, perception changes reception, and reception will change your life.

# 5.  Step Up Your Game

"Yes, that's a dozen roses for English. The room registered to C. English," I confirmed. "Uh-huh. And that'll be delivered first thing in the morning with the voucher, yes? Good. Good night to you, too." I hung up the phone then plopped down on the edge of the bed, skimming the entire top floor suite.

"Look at yourself Maurice. You, her, the city, the meal, the bracelet. All of it was all perfect and yet, here you sit. Alone. Again," I said aloud, looking at my reflection in the mirror attached to the dresser before me. "You're on the upside of your forties and still flubbing when it comes to getting what you want in the woman department."

I had returned from what should've been a nice dinner, gotten comfortable, fixed myself a stiff drink comprised of a majority of the contents kindly left by the hotel staff in the mini bar, and was hosting a pretty good pity party with yours truly as the guest of honor. I was completely disgusted with myself.

"Instead of settling into a bubble bath in that Jacuzzi tub fifteen feet away, or her sleeping next to you, she's settling into her own room, planning on heading back to Baltimore in the morning." *Maybe she's right. Maybe I am a thick-skulled idiot.*

In case you're wondering, the *she* I am referring to is none other than Ms. Cassidy English. We met about seven months back. She's an attractive woman, there's no doubt about that, but it's more than her physical beauty that attracts me to her. It's the way that she listens to me, the way that she looks up to me. She respects me and what I do, and actually thinks I have something to teach and offer her. My wife used to look at me in a lot of those same ways, which I miss, and I just honestly enjoy being in Cassidy's presence. She's a good confidant. A comfort, I guess. But she's hard to figure out. One day, we're great. The next, she's pushing me away. Still, she is my student, my infatuation. As for what led to the pity party, well I can't tell you exactly. All I can tell you is what happened.

Cassidy and I flew out to California two days ago. We came to Napa Valley on "business". By that I mean I came to speak and demonstrate at a special convention at The Copia. She *thought* she came to schmooze with some of the top chefs in the nation and to pick up a thing or two to help her career. By the way, we're both chefs; me with 20 years under my belt and she with just three. But really, I brought her along thinking that getting her out of our usual atmosphere and everything we were accustomed to back home in Baltimore would finally allow me to get close to her the way I wanted.

I'm a planner. And just like I always do, I planned this trip with flawless calculation, or at least I thought I did. After finding out that the host hotel for the convention was going to give me a complimentary room for the duration of the convention, five days in all, I negotiated to do a special presentation for the hotel's guests in exchange for an upgrade to the most lavish suite available. Cassidy and I would be sharing the suite, of course. Once I scored that, I continued planning out the week, making sure something special was arranged for Cassidy each day. Wednesday, it was meeting Emeril. Yesterday, it was a day of hands-on advanced pastry designing at The Culinary Institute of America with a bunch of fancy-schmancy folks from overseas she's always raving about—Denmark, I think—followed by a facial and stone therapy massage at the hotel spa. The special surprise for today was dinner at one of the better restaurants in town, Don Giovanni. Tonight was also supposed to be the night she graciously received the ebony-encircled, Italian marble hinge bracelet I designed and had custom-made for her. But as you know, I ended up in the suite alone. So, obviously, that plan didn't go over so well. I don't understand why, but hey, it is what it is.

So we're at the restaurant and everything is going rather smoothly. Nice dinner; She had the lobster and I went for the Venison. She talked about her day. I listened. Everything was fine until a woman, who must have been on staff at The Copia, came by and spilled the news that all of Puck's (as in Wolfgang Puck) apprenticeship interviews had been filled. Cassidy nearly spit her red wine across the entire table. Knowing that this was uncharacteristic behavior for Cassidy English, who was always the proper lady, I knew dinner was about to take a turn towards the undesirable.

Cassidy, like she had done so many other times before, looked me dead in my face, silently searching my eyes. I, as I always did, began to cast my eyes in any other direction but she, as she always did, whispered a forceful "don't" through her clenched teeth. She then leaned forward and motioned with her right hand forefinger for me to come closer. "You *did* secure my interview with Wolfgang Puck for tomorrow, didn't you?" she questioned. "Because you know how important the interview is, beyond all of the other things I've asked of you in the past, because it's what I need to get to where I want to be, right?"

I sat there wondering what I should do. *Do I tell her that I never put the call in to Puck or do I lie, call him an egotistical butcher who doesn't deserve to have someone as talented as her working under him and say, 'of course I got you an interview' then pay one of the interviewees off so Cassidy can have their spot and interview? Lie. The lie sounds good...except she's gotten pretty good at reading me over the last couple months. She might know. Crap. The truth it is, but I'll sugarcoat it to make it seem like she's better off.*

"I...uh...yeah, I didn't contact him...at all. You see," I rushed on, "I was pretty sure he would still be upset over this cook-off we had back in '89 at which I kind of adjusted his oven and his quiche came out slightly charred…anyway, I was fairly certain he wouldn't even look at your file once he discovered that I am your mentor and the one providing your recommendation. I'm sorry Cassidy. I was young," I finished taking a sip of my wine.

Cassidy adjusted in her seat, straightening her back as she took in a deep breath the way people do when they're highly disturbed over something but want to keep their composure. "So what you're saying is that I will have to wait another nine months before I have this opportunity again because you and Puck can't play nice? Because of some stupid culinary prank nearly 20 years ago?" she asked calmly.

"Only if you decided to wait on Puck. You know that you could get the same, if not better, experience if you would just take me up on my offer and work under me," I said. *Under, on top, I'd be happy either way.*

"You know I wouldn't…" I began.

"Yes you would," she replied.

"Well, word is, Puck always leaves a wildcard spot open. I'll get you in front of him Sunday. We're both doing that demonstration at The Copia at 2:00pm. Be my assistant and you'll be able to chatter away at him the entire time," I countered. "Let me help. I don't mind."

"Maurice, I know you want to help me. At least you say it time and time again to me."

"Cassidy, I do want to help you but you won't let me…"

"Right," she said with a disbelieving sigh.

"No really, I will…"

"I know that the things that you want to do I don't need— paying my bills, trying to keep me sexed up, wanting to take me on vacations. It's not necessary. But when I ask you to do the things that *I* desire like writing recommendations, teaching me things to enhance my skills or doing what you say you are going to do, you fall short."

"Cassidy, I do it because you do so much more for me. I just..."

"We have a friendship. How 'bout we leave it at that," she cut in.

"What do you...Why?"

"Because I can't count on you, Maurice. At least, not for the important stuff." Cassidy bowed her head, let out a short laugh, and began shaking her head from side to side.

"I *am* sorry. I *will* fix things. Promise. And I need you to know I don't mean to let you down. I just..."

"What is it Maurice, huh? Why can't you ever do what you say you'll do?" she asked, her voice squeaking and her fork dropping to her plate.

"Take it easy, Cassidy. I said I would follow through," I said with a whisper and leaning in towards her. I glanced around the restaurant then realizing no one was paying us much attention, I leaned back and wiped my mouth with my embroidered linen napkin. "Look, I got you something," I said pulling out a purple satin box and laying it on the table. "Consider it a peace offering."

Cassidy didn't even look at the box. She just let it sit on the table. "Maurice, I've told you this a thousand times before. I don't need...no...I don't *want* jewelry from you. I don't want money from you. I don't want anything from you. I'm not your woman. You have a wife. I am your mentee and your friend. That is all."

"Cassidy, I know that I'm married. I'm the one who stood up at the altar with Jessica. I see her every single day. And I'm the one who's teaching you what you didn't learn in culinary school. Me. I'm the one with twenty years in the business. I know where we stand."

"Really? Because you don't always act like it. I know that nothing romantic is going to happen between us on this trip, but how does your wife feel about you and me sharing a suite? Does she even know?"

"What's between my wife and I is none of your business," I said pushing the box towards her. "And as I was saying, the gift which, since you've neglected to open it I guess I'll tell you is a one-of-a-kind bracelet, I just thought you'd like it."

"Why?"

"Why what?" I asked.

"Why did you buy me a bracelet? It's not my birthday. I haven't saved your life. It's just Friday," she rambled off.

"I saw it and it seemed like it'd suit you. Friends do that for friends."

She picked up the box, took the bracelet out and inspected it. "What is that, ebony? And marble? Awfully expensive gift for a friend and I've certainly never seen you give anything so extravagant to your other female friends or your men friends," she began. After studying the bracelet further, she read the inscription aloud, "'To my Cassidy' it reads," she said looking up at me.

"They must have botched it. Left out the word friend. It was supposed to read 'To my friend Cassidy'," I responded. *I didn't mean anything by it. She is mine. My mentee. My friend who's a girl.* "Why do you have a problem with the inscription…or the bracelet for that matter? It was meant as a kind gesture."

"A kind, friendly gesture is fine. But this, this is more than that…or at least it feels like it was meant to be. Anyway, we've been through this before," she began. "I don't even want to discuss it tonight."

"No. You brought it up," I pushed, "so let's discuss it."

"You paid my car note last month."

"And?"

"And I didn't ask you to. As I recall, all I asked for was for you to loan me a couple dollars for gas."

"I figured if you didn't have gas money you probably didn't…"

"That's beside the point. It was too much. You're not my father. You're not my man. It wasn't your place. I'm still trying to figure out how you did that."

"Well, I didn't mean to…I only wanted to help and…" I began.

"Or what about back when we first met? Trying to pay for manicures and pedicures for my girlfriends and me. I barely knew you then and you certainly didn't know my friends. The flowers…"

"Well, I…"

"…Checking on me to make sure I get home okay, and…"

"Well now, that's just being courteous. You're a pretty young woman and there are too many crazy people out there. That's a friend checking on a friend," I rebutted.

"Okay, I'll give you that one but what about the time you sent me lingerie or the time you cornered me in the test kitchen…"

"I apologized for my inappropriate behavior on those occasions."

"You did, but you keep doing the same things over and over and over again. You do something. I tell you I don't like it. You fix it then a couple weeks later, you do something else to piss me off. And what makes it so bad is I know you're not stupid. Matter-of-fact, I think you know what's going to make me mad, either by you doing that thing or in this case, not doing it."

"That's ridiculous. Why would I intentionally…"

"I have no clue. Maybe you have blinders on or some-thing," she replied, with exasperation. "Don't get me wrong, Maurice. I appreciate the things you've done for me—the come-ons being an exception, but I could care less about them, especially the material things. I'm not in your life because of that. It's you. You, and the man that you are, are what keep me in your life. But for some reason, you still insist on all this other stuff."

"So what do you want?"

"You know me well enough by now. I shouldn't have to tell you but it's obvious I do. Case in point: I accepted your invitation to come to Napa because I thought it would be fun to be out here with you, colleague to colleague, and yes, I admit I was hoping the trip would be a good place for me to network too. But really all I wanted from you was to spend time, learn a thing or two, and if you could manage it, for you to help me get in good with Wolfgang. We've had fun, but you let me down on Wolfgang. Instead of focusing your efforts on that, you went off, probably planning a whole trip itinerary to 'keep me happy' but do I look happy? No. Because the one thing I asked for, the one thing I needed, you didn't do. And what makes it so bad is this has become a cycle. I'm tired of it, Maurice, and I have to wonder if this friendship is worth all the fatigue," she said standing up and tossing her napkin onto the chair.

"Sit down, Cassidy," I said sharply. My eyes darted back and forth sideways. I was convinced she was causing a scene that would attract an audience. "I will contact Puck's manager tonight. He owes me a favor. I will get you the interview with Puck."

Still standing, Cassidy tossed her head back slowly and laughed lightly. "See. This is exactly what I'm talking about. Why did it have to come to this? Why all the games? Why couldn't you have just done what I asked the first time around if it was that simple instead of concocting this whole scene with the dinner and the bracelet and whatever else you had up your sleeve? Why must I always check you before you'll do what I need?"

"Sit down, Cassidy," I said tossing my napkin onto my plate.

"I will not. Nor will I be finishing out my trip with you. I'm going back to the hotel, gathering my things and getting my own room and…"

"You can't afford a room at the…"

"I can't afford not to get my own room. I need some space. Some time to rethink this friendship," she finished.

"Cassidy, tell me what you want and I will do it."

"Not likely," she said picking up her purse.

After that, Cassidy walked directly out of the restaurant. *She'll forgive me tomorrow. I'll make sure of it. I'll call Puck's manager when I get back and phone Cassidy in the morning with the good news about the interview. Oh, and to really win her back, a voucher for a full day at the spa…and a dozen red, no,* yellow *roses.* I paid the waiter, had him wrap up the desserts we'd pre-ordered then headed to the hotel. By the time I got there, she had already gotten her bags from our room and was at the front desk arranging for a room of her own. I started to walk up to her, but stopped mid-stride. *Why should I go over there? She walked out on me and made me look silly in that restaurant. Besides, I'm not in the mood to argue anymore tonight. Maybe her being alone for the night will do her some good; show her how ridiculous she's being and that she should be appreciative of the things I do for her. I'll just talk to you in the morning, Cassidy.*

## Analysis

As spiritual beings we are drawn to one another and as human beings we need one another. However, because we are raised up in the desires of our flesh we sometimes become confused by the desires of our heart. We find ourselves attracted to others and unaware that attraction does not always have to manifest itself in a sexual expression. But because we do not have ready access to role models who have mastered effective relationships, we are unable to interpret the signals that are sent to us. We need to understand that it is possible to have an appreciation for someone without having to consummate it sexually. Even friendships have an initial attraction that has to exist to draw the two together, regardless of gender. We have to learn how to allow ourselves to enjoy attraction to others and enjoy it in platonic fashion, allowing life to reveal to you the blessing that the relationship has for you.

When people are drawn to your gifts, it is not for you to use those people as Maurice did with Cassidy, to take advantage of them. It is actually an indicator that you are demonstrating the innate gift that God has given you. You can misuse your gifts and be blind to the rewards that they can provide to you. It is important that in the use of your gifts, you also balance them with a positive self outlook. When you appreciate who you are in your God Essence and are not suffering from the inadequacies of your ego, you find no need to use people to prove to yourself that you are worthy. You will no longer have the desire to prove to yourself that you are superior in any way. Your main focus will be one of unity rather than separation. In this way, you will see that the old wounds of your past will heal and a sense of peace and purpose will permeate your life. The goal then will be to be a person of integrity; one without the limitations of the flesh. You find that when you feel good about yourself, you want everyone else to feel good as well. It becomes unimportant that you have the upper hand with anyone else or that you have the ability to one-up the next guy.

Life is not about how much you acquire, and yet when you live life in order, there is nothing that you *can't* acquire. If you have to lie to prove a point, you don't have a point. And a lie can show itself in many ways: outright deceit, omission, or manipulation, just to list a few. But a mark of a powerful person is someone who can say what they want and bring it in to fruition without trickery. Most of us subscribe to the idea that what is for us *is* for us and there is no way to avoid it. Well if we truly believe this, why is it necessary to use deception to bring it about? Furthermore, if you find something or someone that you want to have in your space, why not value, respect and appreciate whatever it was that attracted it to you in the first place, and allow yourself to enjoy it?

When you find people like Maurice using his position to lure women in, and then not coming through, (and then claiming he doesn't know "why" they're upset with him) you should know that he is suffering from lack of self worth. When someone knows that they are of value, they know that they do not have to fool people into being interested in them. When you find someone who makes promises to help another and then refuses (or "forgets") to do so, it is because they want to take from the person without giving in return, usually following a sick cycle that was perpetrated on them.

People, it is important that you watch for the tell-tale signs and look out for the "users" in the world. Everyone is on their journey, but that does not mean that you have to allow them in your space as they proceed. I'm not saying *condemn* them, because they, like you, are doing the best they can with what they have. I'm saying: bless them as they continue on their way but be sure to make yourself scarce when you see them coming!

When a person feels the need to have to conquer another, this is an indication that they have a need to personally search their souls for answers. Consider this a warning indicator from the internal navigational system that all of us have within. This person needs to become aware of their personal self worth. Self worth is not found in the conquering of others. It is found in the respect and value of self. You must first realize that disrespect and devaluing others does not bring value to you. Nor will it heal the wounds that exist within you. The ability to win over another will *not* prove to the world or yourself that you are important. This is why, even after continued practice of these behaviors, you still cannot achieve the sense of accomplishment or wholeness that you seek.

If you try to acquire someone only because you think that person will elevate your image in the eyes of others, you will be willing to use any means necessary to "get" that person, and for a while you might feel pretty pleased in having accomplished that goal. Now, when you love and care for someone who also just happens to elevate your image, there's nothing wrong with this because you also respect that other person's true value separate from what they can do for you. But if you're only trying to get with that person BECAUSE you think they will be able to boost you, then that's where the problem lies. You will find that victory to be empty because it was selfishly motivated, like the case of Maurice and Cassidy. This is just another feeble attempt to find a sense of wholeness outside of self with ego justification. This won't work; it is just a dog that won't walk.

Instead of spending a lot of time fighting the natural process of life and trying to succeed playing by your own manipulative rules. Why don't you stop, examine the situation, develop a new plan for success that does not involve manipulating others, implement it, and watch how amazing your life will become. People who operate like Maurice never seem quite happy. They appear to have it all and yet are never at peace, and they don't even understand it themselves. Successful life will not allow you to play both sides of the fence and get the reward. You have to pick a master and serve it with dedication to achieve success. If you find someone that you feel could possibly be of value in your life or that has a special effect on you, first ask your self why you feel that way. Is it because you will appear cool to your friends or because of what you think they can "do" for you? If so, this is an ego-motivated feeling and is sure to create negative consequences. Or, is this person appealing to you because you feel as though you could have a special bond with him or her, one that will allow you to evolve together to a higher level? If so, this is an Essence-motivated feeling and should be pursued.

What if someone peaks your curiosity because the male in you (even if you're a woman) loves a "challenge", and you crave an opportunity to rise to the challenge and prove that you can be victorious? This is an ego-driven motivation and again will give you only unsatisfactory results. And what if you meet someone and you feel that their very presence inspires you to be the best that you can be? Then this is an Essence-motivated feeling and will prove to be an experience loaded with rewards beyond your wildest imagination.

Don't be an accomplice with your flesh to impede your spiritual progress. Check yourself so that no one else can check you. Become the observer of your life and actions. Ask yourself why you do the things that you do. Don't allow yourself to make ego-motivated choices, because these are the choices that create the darkness in your life.

Treat people the way that you want to be treated. Yes, it's the old Golden Rule. Keep in mind that every action has a reaction. What you put out there will eventually come back to you, whether it is good or bad. You have a choice, so why not choose the good: discipline yourself to discontinue the behaviors that don't create the lasting benefits for your life.

Know that most of the time it is the unpopular decisions that in the end make you respected. Note that the stand-out person is not the person doing what everyone else is doing, because then they are not standing out, they are just blending in. I understand that everyone wants to be special, but the key to realizing true contentment is this: believing that you are *already* special, being your true self, and allowing life to show you where your specialness lies. Believe me, it is a lot less taxing doing it this way, and in any event you will find that after trying everything else, it is the only way that truly works. Make no mistake about it, you will come to this in the end because life won't let go until you get it right. So you can go gracefully or you can go scratching and kicking, but make no mistake you will go. The choice of how you do it is up to you, and ladies and gentlemen—this is what free will is. What will your choice be?

# 6.  Dangle and Don't Deliver

*So I'll just go in, say what I gotta say, and that'll be that. What will my mother say though? My boys? Naw, They won't find out. Remember: He's a perfect stranger so it won't get back to anyone I know. It'll be fine. Just chattin' with a fella. That's all. Just gotta get it out of my system is all and I'll be good as new. Back to my usual self. All right. No worries. None. All right then, let's do this.*

Sufficiently psyched up, I hopped out of my car and headed into the mirrored glass, 12-story building in front of me. As I walked into the door, I spotted the elevator and stairwell. I took a deep breath, loosened my tie, then headed up the steps towards the fourth floor. I stepped through the door to the fourth floor into an open, contemporary area. *Nagaya...Nagaya...suite 437 should be...to the right.* I walked down the hallway until I reached the door that said Nagaya. It was a gray metal door and I could see my reflection in it, except it wasn't my normal reflection. My reflection was kind of skewed, like when you look at yourself in one of those fun house mirrors. *Figures. He would have a door that's reflective so you have to take a look at yourself before entering.* I stood there in front of the door, moving from side to side trying to see if there was any position or angle at which I could stand to look normal, like myself. It was useless. The only things that looked normal in my reflection were my eyes and the sad part about that was my eyes were the last things I wanted to see clearly because as they say, the eyes are the windows to the soul and I knew I wasn't ready for the view.

I saw my ex fiancé, Bianca, four months ago. We ran into one another at the buffet table during my brother's wedding reception. I was apprehensive when I first saw her—we hadn't parted on the best of terms—but she looked wonderful, better than when we were together and for some reason, I wanted to speak. Big mistake. We went through the typical fake, get reacquainted conversation—career and family updates, what old friends are up to, etc. When we spoke she was cordial but cold; not at all how I remembered her. But once the faux pleasantries were through, the conversation turned. I remember what she said verbatim. She said, "This is the wedding you promised me back when we were dating; the place, the feel. Good plan, just no follow through. Worked out for the best though. I'm happier now and you," she paused right then, looked me over, stopped when she got to my ring-less left hand, then drove the nail straight into my heart saying, "well you're...still you." Yeah. You heard right. She basically called me a pitiful, lonely, lying cad. Yeah, she had balls.

My initial reaction was that she was just trying to be mean and that to make it really sting she purposely did it in an empathetic way. I would've figured that after six years she would have been okay. Especially since she was standing there with a rock the size of Gibraltar on her finger and a cute gent at her side, presumably her husband, but I guess not. Still, she got me to thinking. Had I really been that bad to her? And if I had treated her so badly, the woman that I had loved the most out of them all, what did that say about how I'd treated other women who followed? I didn't know what to think—maybe because a part of me agreed with her. I don't know.

For the most part I think I'm a decent guy. I work hard. I love my mother. I even do community service sometimes. I've got a hold on most things in my life, except relationships with women; they're always so complicated. It didn't used to be that way. Back when I was in college things were actually pretty simple but I don't know if it was because I wanted less or if the women I was dealing with expected less. What I do know is those were the good days. My sisters used to call me the Callous Casanova because, according to them, I went through women so fast and didn't treat them right. I disagree with them totally. The relationships were just what they were.

There was this one girl, Madison. She was a really sweet girl. Unlucky for her I realized early on that she was naïve and easily manipulated. I had her doing all sorts of things for me. She wasn't even my girlfriend but I made it seem like she could be a contender. I had her doing my laundry and cooking meals for me on Sunday so I could eat for the rest of the week. Didn't pay for groceries either. It was all good at first but then I began to feel like she was doing it because she was trying to gain popularity—I *was* pretty popular at school—but after a while that got old to me and I really didn't appreciate being used like that so I cut her loose. Did it at her sorority's spring soiree. I was supposed to be her escort for the debutante court or whatever but I never showed. Dumped her via text message. I *know* I was on Madison's sh\*t list—probably still am. I didn't care though. Madison ended up being the first of many. You'd think college co-eds would be smart enough not to fall for stuff like I had Madison doing, but every year I found a new handmaiden—that's what I called them, because they were at my beck and call. But truth is, I got a lot more from my handmaidens than clean laundry and some good down home cooking. I learned about women. I learned that if I talked to them right, I could have just about everything without having to give anything.

Crystal was my transition girl—the one who I was with when I graduated college and for a year and half after. At that point, I was so focused on my career and getting my investments going that having her around was really more out of convenience than anything. Anyway, she drunk-dialed me one night. Crystal was screaming through the phone saying I made her mutilate her body, which was absolutely untrue, and that her self-esteem is in the crapper because of "how I treated her, how I led her on". Though she was a little hysterical, I know she meant every word she said. After all, people are the most honest when they're drunk. But I had been with the girl for over two years. She knew who I was. It wasn't my fault if she chose to see me as what *she* wanted me to be. She did that. Just like she researched the doctor and saved the money and drove herself to the appointment. She chose to have her breast done. All I did was tell her she'd be the kind of girl that a man would marry, especially if she had bigger breasts because she had everything else going for her but that. I just wasn't that sexually attracted to her with the breasts she had. I never thought she'd go through with it though. I thought she'd cuss me out and leave me before she did any of that but she didn't. I mean, she really didn't have any reason to stay in the relationship. Looking back, I was just going through the motions. Like I said, I was focused on my career so I wasn't around much and though I was making more than I ever had in college, I really didn't spend it on her...just enough to keep her content so I could keep up my sex life and have an escort for this business event and that one. The doctor did do a good job on her breasts—they looked good, were fun to play with—it was just that by then, I'd kind of checked out on the relationship.

Since her, I've been whipping through women left and right. If I had to commit to them in some way or promise them something to get what I wanted, I did. I got mine until I got tired of them, things started to get complicated, or they wised up and moved on. Regardless of how the relationship ended, it never fazed me for long. Sure it was heated at times, depending on how things ended. I *did* care for the women to some degree...I wouldn't have had relationships with them if I didn't...but I never dwelled over the relationships long because I knew that there would always be another woman to fill her spot. Like I said earlier, I learned a lot about women when I was in college and as an adult, the only thing I learned was that no matter how old the woman, the same rules applied: She wants to feel special and cared for and as long as I can create that illusion, no matter how dedicated *(or not)* that I am to making the fantasy real, she'll stick around. I don't know if it's an innate thing or what but all the women I've been with hold on tight when they see a glimmer of hope of getting what they want. Good or bad, it's worked for me all my life.

Bianca was the one that was different though. I fed her the same bull, created the same illusion but somehow, with her, I actually found myself believing it too and wanting to be the man she wanted me to be. It was a weird feeling. Like I said, most of the women I dealt with, I made all sorts of plans, promises, noble gestures, whatever to get them to do what I wanted...and I did the same with her; but deep down, I knew part of me meant the things I was doing for her or saying to her. Hell, I even found myself doing things even though they were more for *her* benefit than mine. I admit talking seriously with her about us getting married, making actual plans on the type of wedding, a trip to the jewelry store—not just a strategic trip to the jewelry store to bait her into doing something I wanted later or to keep her docile, but a real trip to see what she liked. I felt good, like the relationship was right. Satisfied would be the word to describe it I guess, but at the same time, I felt like I was losing myself-almost like she was slowly chipping away at who I was. After all, she was really no different than most of the others. I just could not figure out what was going on. Hell, I don't know, maybe I was just getting old. So, I did what any other man in his right mind would do. I grabbed the brick and mortar and put up a wall. I took my heart out of the equation and 74 days later, she was gone. That was the first time I was truly sad to see a relationship end; the first time I ever really questioned my actions in the relationship. And when it was over, I wasn't mad; I was, well I don't think I felt anything. I was numb. In retrospect, the chiseling she did probably wasn't a bad thing but at that time, I couldn't deal.

Still standing in front of the mirrored door, studying my reflection, I couldn't help but wonder where I would be if I hadn't let my own mind get the best of me, if I had just let the relationship unfold without all the mind games, if I could have just given up control and left things to fate. *How different would my life be now?* I looked around. The hallway was void of all life, all noise. *This is what it has come to; I messed myself up so much I can't even figure me out anymore. I knew I didn't mean what I said to most of those women when the words crossed my lips. I knew I was leading them on. All the promises broken. And what makes it so bad is that I got so good at it. The question is, why? Why did I do it? Why do I do it?*

"Hell, if I knew that, I wouldn't be here. That's for damn sure," I blurted out at my reflection. *I should be able to figure this out or control my actions. Yeah, I can...but I haven't...But I will. I can do it myself. I can figure this out for myself. I mean, I do know my actions haven't gotten me to be where I really want to be. I definitely don't want to be a bachelor all my life. So what do I need some doctor for? I don't. I'm out of here.* As I turned to leave I heard my keys drop to the floor beside me. I picked them up and headed for the elevator but before I got ten feet down the hall, I heard a voice call my name.

"Mr. Harris?"

*Damn.* I turned around and nodded with a forced smile. "Yes, that's me. Dr. Nagaya?"

"In the flesh! Come on in. Have a sit down on the sofa. The chair's mine," he said with a gruff laugh.

The voice had come from a tall, rotund man with wire frame glasses who was peeking out from the office door by which I had been standing. He had a small tape recorder in one hand and half a corned beef sandwich in the other. *So this is the man that's supposed to help me with my wicked, wicked ways. We'll see about that.*

## Analysis

My observations of men and women have led me to believe that when it comes to commitment for men, it is the assumed right *time*, and for women it is the assumed right *man*. With women, the man is the one that they think will be able to make the dream truth and they are willing to pay the price for it to happen. With men, when they realize that their actions of ego-feeding leave them weary and unfulfilled, they just want to settle down and try something a little different, and whoever is in their space at the time that they think is remotely worthy, becomes the one. This sounds so ugly, but it appears to be true.

Mr. Harris thought that Bianca was special. Not because of Bianca, but because of where he was in his life and what he wanted. The thing that we have to come to know is that every reaction that we have is *not* based on the person that we are reacting to. It has everything to do with *us*, our feelings that we bring to the situation and project onto the person. For example, you think that someone is beautiful or handsome; your opinion is based on your years of association and programming as to what those terms mean to you. That is why we find certain people attractive while others do not, because personal filters and baggage are the variables that create differences in tastes and opinions. The general consensus about someone could be highly favorable, but that person could remind you of an old neighbor that you despised and your opinion of the person could be negative simply based on your frame of reference. Also, this type of experience can happen to you subconsciously and you don't even know at first thought why you feel the way that you do, but upon further contemplation you realize where the actual dislike is coming from. Meanwhile, the person that you are currently projecting onto has no idea but suffers the consequences of your past. See how that works? It had nothing to do with the actual *person*; it had *everything* to do with *you*. And this process can work positively as well as negatively.

Everything that we do as humans, we do in an attempt to get our needs met on some level. When you hear this statement at first it sounds harsh, but it is true. When we are kind to someone, sure we want to help, but we also like the way that it makes us feel or the positive consequences we derive from our kind action.

There is nothing wrong with getting your needs met. The challenge is to know what your true needs are. A tip for you is to know that your true desire will never be selfishly motivated. Therefore, if you are getting your needs met, and someone or something else will also benefit, this is life in balance. But when you get your needs met at the expense of others, the needs that you are satisfying are not your true desires. You will find this to be a fear-motivated need and anything motivated by fear is false and should be eradicated in order that your true desire can be exposed and satisfied.

When you think that you are getting one over on other people, the joke turns out to be on you. Yes, in the present it feels as though life for you is great, but the person or people that you are mistreating are actually getting a lesson (whether they know it or not) that they should be grateful for because it will prove to be highly beneficial to them in the future (and perhaps the lesson is that they should not trust YOU!) For you, you are only being victorious in creating a web that will eventually trap you and lead you to a point of emotional break down; but never fear—that is where you will get your lesson in order to get your blessing. Know that there is a less tumultuous route, and opt for it. There is a consequence for everything that we do, so why not make your consequences positive ones.

When you dangle something that someone desires in front of him in an effort to get him to do something that you want, even though you have no intentions of delivering, know that whatever you have gotten from him, you *stole*. Stealing is taking something that does not belong to you without permission. If someone gives you something under false pretenses, that person is entering into the deal with misinformation and therefore, he is making decisions based on erroneous information. Had the person known your true intentions, would he have made the same choice? The answer is probably no, and you knew that; hence, the belief that you needed to deceive him in order to get your way. This feels cool at first and really pumps the ego, but victory is short lived and has a high price attached.

As you see with Mr. Harris, he thought he had it going on. He even felt as though he was unstoppable, and yet he is scheduling appointments for therapy. Now, I'm not saying that therapy is not necessary in a lot of situations. In fact, I believe it can be beneficial in many people's lives, but if we took time to check ourselves and use some foresight, we would see most of what it is we need to see before we embarked on our missions.

We have become a mentally lazy people. We don't want to take the time to analyze what we want and what we are doing. We have allowed ourselves to mostly lead by feeling—which is the vehicle of the flesh. Yes, it is good to feel, but if you allow your flesh to lead, you will find yourself confined by the limitations of the world because spirit is knowledgeable and full of wisdom. The two can coexist and create a marvelous existence, but ego/flesh motivations cannot dominate and create the same results. Most of us have been warned for a large portion of our lives to think before we do things. And in spite of the warnings, we proceed through life without any forethought whatsoever and then condemn the people that *do* think. We say to people that we find to be mindful, "you think too much, you are too analytical"; but the truth is we don't want them to encourage us to do something that we know that we need to do. We don't want to be reminded that our actions all have a reason because it would require us to take a look at ourselves, and then we might have to condemn who and what we are and what we have done.

Well, the solution to this is to learn to appreciate your experiences as lessons and preparation for your future. Remember that you are a worthy being because you are not your Ego but your Essence, and at The Essence you are God. Then, it will not be so painful to examine yourself and your life, and to make more beneficial and loving decisions on your behalf.

Whatever your goal is in life, you need to have a plan to achieve that end and not develop habits and skills that support something different. Mr. Harris said that he did not want to be a bachelor all of his life, but he is at mid life and he has not developed the skills to support a monogamous reciprocal relationship based in truth and love. Whatever you put in, you get out, and that's the bottom line. So now, at a time when he should be cashing out and reaping the benefits of what he should have sowed earlier, he has to retrain himself in order to develop the practices and habits that will bring him the desires of his heart.

You have to ask yourself these questions: If you knew that such-and-such was your ultimate goal for your life, why did you not spend more time preparing yourself for it? Did you think that the ineffective behaviors that you indulged in would ultimately benefit you? Or did you think your goal would magically manifest itself with no effort on your part? I would say that the answer to that is no. It's a matter of priorities, and if that thing were so important to you, you would have made it your priority sooner.

Sometimes, when we hold something as "ultimate", we do so because we believe it to be the "best" and that it will have to be saved for last, because once you achieve it there is nothing else that can top it in our minds. Of course, this is untrue, because every time we achieve a higher level of experiences and awareness, the unlimited universe will expose us to a higher awareness, it is infinite.

We are committed to the results that we have because if we wanted something different, we would have it. It is not enough to say that we *want* something. When you are passionate about something, you speak it. Then, you act to create and bring it into your reality. You make it a top priority. Don't take my word for it. Look at your own past and ask yourself: When you really wanted something and were committed to it, did it not in fact manifest? Did you not do the work necessary to achieve it or get it? You are a powerful being. You just need to realize, accept, and walk in the awareness of this truth.

# 7.   I Don't Know My Worth

"All right. Now that we're all caught up on the latest gossip, how 'bout you guys tell me what's really going on."

I was having lunch with my friends Thalia and Saundra at a small café off of 77th in Manhattan. It's not that there was anything unusual about us lunching together. What sent up the red flag though was that Thalia had requested the lunch on the spur-of-the-moment, which meant that we ended up at, well, a café. That never happens. We're self-proclaimed cuisine snobs and normally when we get together, we're breaking in the hottest restaurant that has opened that month so I knew something was up. I smelled man trouble. That was usually the reason for our impromptu lunches and somehow, over the years, I had become the Dr. Ruth, Dr. Jacque in my case, of our click. I didn't mind the title but I did think it was kind of strange. To me, Thalia and Saundra were the ones who really had themselves together. Unlike me, both of them were college-educated and phenomenal women in their own way. Thalia, a striking 5'10" Puerto Rican & Black beauty, is an Art Director for one of the largest advertising agencies in New York. She is smart, creative and on the fast track to becoming the youngest, and only minority, Creative Director at the company. Saundra, though gorgeous enough to win a runway walk-on with Naomi Campbell, is a photographer—her passion is shooting life moments. She hasn't hit it big yet but after getting one of her pictures picked up by *Time* last month, I'm sure she'll be well on her way soon. And me, well I have always been the cute friend of the pretty girls. I own a small bakery in Harlem. Emphasis on *small* but it's mine.

"Oh, so our house psychiatrist is here, ready to prescribe advice, huh?" Thalia teased.

"Sure am. Dish," I said, taking one last bite of my Blueberry Cheesecake.

"Well Dr. Jacque, Perry…," Thalia began.

"Is he still talking about wearing Jordans and a Kobe jersey for your ceremony? Don't trip. You've still got time to change his mind," I said laughing.

"Jacque, this is serious," Saundra chimed in.

"Sorry. Go ahead," I said pushing my plate to the edge of the table and straightening up in my chair.

"Well, you know I've been trying to get right with God. It's going well. I'm growing spiritually and prospering at work but things at home, they still haven't gotten any better. I've long since stopped trying to get Perry to go to Bible study with me but now he's saying that I'm neglecting him because I'm at the church so much," she explained.

"Well, you knew he wasn't religious when you met him," I said.

"Yes, I knew. And I'm not trying to change that but I was just hoping that he would support me in my efforts to learn more about God and myself spiritually," she continued. "He was fine for the first couple months but now it's almost like he's purposely trying to stop me from going all together…"

"The last three weeks he's had to *work* overtime," Saundra interjected sarcastically, "conveniently at the times she'd normally be going to Saturday Fellowship. Tell her Thalia."

"Yes, he's done that. I still went, just called one of the sisters from the church to pick me up," she continued.

"Well, wha…," I began.

"That's not all. Last Sunday when I got ready to go to church, the seat was pushed all the way back, further than what Perry needs to drive. I didn't think anything of it but as I was driving into the church parking lot, I hit a speed bump and an empty bottle of Hypnotiq and a bottle of pineapple massage gel rolled out from under the seat," she said starting to tear up. "I think that he might be…"

"Thalia. Come on now. Did you ask him?" I asked abruptly.

"No. I've just been praying over it and…," she began reasoning, tears rolling down her cheek.

"Ask him," I said reaching inside my purse. I pulled out my compact mirror and shoved it in front of her. "This is what not knowing is doing to you." She looked at her reflection then bowed her head, shaking it from side to side slowly. "I'm not saying that praying over it is the wrong thing to do but you need to know. God may give you an answer on Perry, if you're asking the right question, but it may not be in the time you want. You're supposed to be marrying this man in two and a half months. Why would you go into a marriage with that question in the back of your mind? And did you ever think about what your marriage is going to be like? He doesn't even respect you trying to enhance *your* spiritual growth. What do you think it's going to be like when kids enter the picture? How do you think that's going to work seeing as though you guys aren't on the same accord spiritually now?"

"I know you're right. My sisters said the same thing but…"

"But nothing Thalia. What is it that makes him so great? What's making you stay with him? Why can't you see that you deserve more?"

"That is true, Girl. I think you should ask him too," Saundra added. "And maybe reconsider the marriage. Is he just someone you can live with or someone you can't live without?"

"I know. I know. I'm going to ask him. I am going to ask Perry. This weekend," Thalia said, lifting her head and nodding as if she were giving herself a pep talk rather than speaking to us. She picked up the mirror and sighed, "Crap. I have a meeting with IBM in forty-five minutes and after all this sister-girl talk I'm going to look puffy. Anybody have any Warm Spirit Herbal Mist?"

"You know I'm always carryin'," I said laughing and reaching into my bag once again. "So are we all better now?"

"Nope," Thalia rang out before Saundra could finish forming her 'yes'.

"Saundra, what's going on with you?" I said, swiveling my chair in her direction.

"It's nothing, really. Money's tight lately 'cause I had to bail Craig out of jail again," she said fidgeting with her straw wrapper.

"Ecstasy or weed?" I asked taking a sip of my Raspberry Tea.

"Both," she answered clearing her throat. "And because…"

"How?" I asked.

"What?" she said, looking confused.

"How did he get caught this time?" I repeated.

"Oh. They picked him up at the Bronx Zoo."

"The zoo?" Thalia and I repeated in unison.

"Yeah. They picked him up around 2 o'clock after he kept trying to climb into the African Plains exhibit. Police say he kept saying he wanted to 'feel like he was on Safari' and 'get a peacock feather so he could tickle his tummy' and that's why he needed to get in there. That tipped the cops off right then that he was on X. Then when they searched him, they found X and a bag of weed. They called it in, pulled him up in the system and a couple hours later, he was in lock-up."

"Mind you, at 2 pm he was supposed to be at his drug addiction support group," Thalia piped in. "You know they let him off his job every week early just to go to that. Makes you wonder if he's been to any of the meetings, doesn't it."

"Thalia!" Saundra exclaimed.

"An eye for an eye Saundra," she responded.

"To make a long story short," Saundra continued, glaring at Thalia, "because this isn't his first offense, he's looking at some hefty lawyer fees and fines that I…"

"Stop right there," I said closing my eyes and holding up my hand. "I know you are not planning on putting yourself in debt over this man," I said emphatically.

"Well, it's just that he helped me out with the rent a few months back when I was between gigs, before I got my pieces in the art gallery. I was…"

"You don't owe that bum a thing. And even if you *thought* you did, you should call it even after just bailing him out."

"Tell it Dr. Jacque!" Thalia said laughing and taking a sip of her Root Beer. "I told her she needed to drop that man. He is nothing but dead weight."

"No doubt, I said shaking my head. "Craig has lied to you…I know you wouldn't have let him stay up in your house if you knew he was still doing drugs…he's spending your money, eating your food and what makes it so bad, he isn't even your man is he?"

"Well…," she hesitated.

"Tell the truth," I pushed. "That man does not claim you as his woman, does he?"

"Not in so many words," she answered.

"Do you need this?" I said sliding the compact over to her. "Open it up and I guarantee you'll see you were not born yesterday. You've only been with the man four months; and I know the sex isn't *that* good, regardless of his self professed sexual talent. Saying it's so don't make it so, you know what I mean? Besides, you are not the kind of woman who has to put up with that mess just to have a man in your life. Cut your losses, today."

Thalia's cell phone began to play, *For the Love of Money* by the O'Jays. "That's my cue ladies. Got to get back to work," she said sliding her chair back and picking up her purse.

"Me too," Saundra said standing up. "I have a buyer coming by in an hour that's interested in the *Life Less Home* piece."

"I should be getting back too. I'd fire me if I were some regular employee who stayed out to lunch this long," I said laughing aloud. "Dump him. The threat of jail time might do Craig some good."

"I'll think about it, okay?" Saundra said pushing in her chair.

"Hardheaded," Thalia mumbled under her breath wrapping her scarf around her neck. "You can do so much better."

"Thalia, I know you're hopping the subway," Saundra began, "but Jacque, did you want to share a cab?"

"No. Go ahead," I said putting my faux fur jacket on. "I'm going to check out a possible new vendor a couple blocks over. You guys call me later, though, if you need to talk." *It's funny how easy it is to give advice to someone else and to forget to follow it yourself when you probably need those same words of wisdom.*

Saundra and Thalia headed out the door. I stood up, placed a $4 tip down and began gathering my things off the table. I reached for the compact to put it back in my purse but dropped it on the table, causing it to flip open. I guess I was still thinking about everything that Thalia and Saundra were going through with their men. I reached for it but stopped cold after my reflection, ten times magnified, popped up on the mirror. I looked closely at my eyes, noticing how dull and discolored the skin around them had become and realizing that though I wasn't sharing my secrets with the girls, the toll they were taking on me was starting to show on my face. Looking in the mirror I thought about the kids, my business, everything. Then, for the first time in five years, I thought about myself. *How much longer are you going to stand for this, Jacque? Nothing is ever going to change if you don't do something. And you know the longer you wait, the more dependent he'll make you become. You've got to do something. Stand up for yourself, your dreams.*

The straw that almost broke the camel's back was laid by my husband on October 16th, Sweetest Day. I'd stayed late at my shop to service customers coming in for last minute goodies to give to their loved ones which meant that I was going to owe the sitter overtime. I knew that we couldn't afford it but I really thought staying open the extra hour would have been worth it.

I got home just in time to make my husband's favorite—baked chicken, Cajun seasoned brown rice and broccoli—and I brought home one of my tangy Key Lime pies. I fed the twins some spaghetti that was left over from the day before and shuttled them off to bed so Irving and I could have a romantic evening. I set the dining room table with our wedding china and placed cinnamon scented candles in the silver candlesticks my grandmother had left to me. Irving came home as I was heading to the bedroom to change.

"Where were you?" he asked dropping his briefcase on the hardwood floor in the foyer.

"What?" I said, stepping backwards as he walked towards me.

"I called at 6:30. You didn't answer. Where were you?" he questioned.

"I kept the shop open an hour longer to make some extra cash, seeing as though it's Sweetest Day and all, and…"

"And that meant you picked the girls up late so now I have to shell out another twenty-five bucks for child care, just 'cause you *thought* you could make money," he finished. "You haven't been making money any other time the shop has been open. Why the hell would you think you could do it tonight?"

"Irving I,…I'm sorry. I'll cut back on…"

"Are you stupid? It's been seven months and all that place has been is trouble. I wish you would get it through your head. Did you at least make me dinner tonight?"

"Baked chicken, brown rice and broccoli," I said scooting past him, heading towards the kitchen.

"Finally, you thought of somebody besides yourself," he said sitting down at the dining room table.

"It takes time before a business really takes off. If you just…"

"Honestly Jacque. I don't know what you are thinking sometimes. What about the kids? You're gone all day, letting some stranger raise our children, just because you're trying to hold on to a stupid childhood dream. It's time you grew up and became a part of this family again. What did we agree on?" he asked.

I was in shock. This was not the evening I had in mind and I didn't understand where all this was coming from. Not tonight, at least. We had almost broke even last month.

"When we got married," he continued, "we said four kids. We said they'd be two and a half years apart. The twins are three. We're supposed to be working on the next kid, not getting a business off the ground, which by the way, is a ridiculously long shot considering the number of restaurants…"

"It's a specialty dessert shop," I mumbled.

"Yeah, well, dessert shops are a dime a dozen in New York City, too. Point is I'm not sure it's an investment I'm willing to afford anymore."

"So what are you saying Irving?"

"I'm saying exactly what I said, Jacque. I did not stutter," he said, taking a bite of the chicken. "Jacque, the hot sauce." I walked over to the fridge, grabbed the hot sauce and handed it to him. Even with his mouth full of the meal I had prepared especially for him, he continued to berate me. "I don't even know why I let you start the damn thing. I guess I thought you could handle work and the family or maybe I thought that if I gave you some responsibility, you could actually handle it. But like always, you proved that you can't. And what makes it so bad is that if you had absolutely any business sense, financial smarts, marketing savvy or anything going for you besides a tight ass and the ability to mix some ingredients together and shove them in an oven, this family might actually make some money instead of going into debt."

I didn't realize it but by then I had halfway huddled into the corner, between the refrigerator and the pantry. It was like I was nine years old again and my father was getting on me because I hadn't cleaned up the kitchen right or hadn't put my little brother to bed by the time he got home. I hated that feeling when I was a child. It didn't feel so good then nor does it feel good now.

He had said hurtful things before but there was something in his eyes that night that was different. I was scared. And it wasn't because I thought he was going to hurt me physically but because I knew that he had absolutely no faith in me and definitely didn't respect me. It was clear that he thought the shop was some *thing* to keep me busy until either he convinced me to stay home "like a good wife" or he got me pregnant again and I *had* to stay home which, considering my health and the pregnancy with the twins, would have certainly been the doctor's orders.

I almost left him that night. But then I realized that the store would never survive without him. So I stayed. I told myself it was just until I could figure things out. It didn't feel right but I didn't know what else to do. I was too embarrassed to ask for help or confide in my girlfriends. That day has played in my mind over and over again for the last three months. As angry as it makes me and as obvious it is that my husband isn't going to change, I can't bring myself to leave.

"'At least it didn't break," I heard a scratchy voice say from behind me.

"What?"

"The mirror," she said pointing at the compact. "'At least it didn't break when ya dropped it. Woulda been unlucky, ya know."

"Right," I said taking one last glance in the mirror before tucking it away in my purse. *If only luck were all I needed.*

## *Analysis*

Teachers teach what it is that they most desire or need to learn. Teaching is a reminder to self of what you know, and the love of what you know and believe encourages you to share that information with others. The trick is to be able to accept what it is you are teaching as truth for yourself as well as expecting your students to accept it. See, as being spiritual beings we already know whatever it is we desire to know; we are equipped with everything. We are just on a journey of rediscovery and remembering. Jacque is able to offer effective advice to her friends because she chooses to be open to that part of her divinity and share it with others. But no matter how we resist Spirit's effectiveness in our personal lives, it is readily available for our successful use. We just have to believe it and receive it.

What I find easiest to do when I have a personal issue is to pretend as though it is someone else's issue, and then I am able to see the solution more clearly, because I can get some objective distance this way. Sometimes you can be too close to see exactly what is right in front of your face—it's the old "can't see the forest for the trees" syndrome.

Packaging does not change content, and lack of self worth can dwell within the most beautiful. Self worth really has nothing to do with your physical appearance, but it has every-thing to do with your inner conviction and knowing. I often ask people if they knew that they were heir to a kingdom would their actions and standards be the same as they are today. If their answer is no, and most times it is, I say to them, "Why wouldn't you be the same person?" Well, they become perplexed as they start to realize that the only thing that would be different in that scenario is their opinion of themselves and therefore, the value that they equate to themselves.

Everything starts with the thoughts that you have. The thoughts are your tools for creation. God tells you that if you can think about it, He will give it to you. It works this way because Source makes itself available to you by dwelling *in* you; therefore, you have constant availability to God's Power. The way you are able to use this power is by thinking about and acting upon the thoughts, and creation will follow from this process. The challenge is because God is all encompassing. If you think negative thoughts, you will also produce that which is negative. So, my suggestion is to "use your power for good".

Does it sound like I'm alluding to the possibility that there is no difference between good and bad? Yes, I am. Is that crazy? Well, let me put it to you another way: how is it possible that we can say that killing is wrong, but then it is also permissible to kill someone that we think is a menace to society? So, is killing wrong, or is it wrong only in certain situations? Now, if it is only wrong in certain situations, why do we say that it is wrong to kill? Either it is wrong to kill or it is not. Or...there is another possibility that says that everything is for the good of something, and we have to trust the process of life to reveal our greatest good; and like the good book says, "Count it all good". Therefore, maybe "good vs. bad" isn't as black and white as we sometimes think.

Change has to start with you and in order for it to be effective change, you need to be in touch with your true feelings and know who and what you are within. You will find that this knowing is empowering and will change your outlook on life. When your view of life changes, the actions you take in life change and therefore, the results for your life become more aligned with who you are and what you intend to be. You can read more about these concepts and ways to restructure your mind in *Take Five* (my first book). Change must take place in an environment that facilitates it in order for the change to be smooth and highly effective. Drug addicts cannot rehab in a crack house. If you find yourself around individuals that impede your evolution, regardless of who they are and the position they hold in your life, you must get distance from them-either physical distance or at least emotional distance. In most cases this seems difficult, but wherever there is a will there is a way and sometimes you have to say no to good to say yes to great.

After you realize that you are a magnificent being, in situations such as Jacque's, the next thing you have to do is to remember that your current situation is created by you. Then realize that if you want something different, *you* must be the one who creates it. You just have to be willing to release the past to embrace the future and the universe will make a way out of no way. You see, this is a really powerful statement that most of us just throw around all willy-nilly, without truly understanding the meaning. In order for something that does not exist to exist, it must be created from the *nothing* and as long as you have *something,* you can't create from the nothing. You have to let go of all that you think you have and then miraculously, creation will happen. If you don't like what you currently have and you can't see another way, know that by just being willing to walk away from what you have, you will make room for something that you could never imagine to exist. I promise you that it will surpass your wildest dreams because your wildest dreams are limited by your knowledge base and the Universe can amaze you because It is infinite knowledge and power.

Whenever we start trying to control and manipulate things to the best of our ability, we have to remember that our ability is small and limited. The key to being victorious in situations is to know that if you trust in the Universe and allow it to perform on your behalf, It will show up and show out because It will not have you in the way throwing up roadblocks. You say, "What do I do with myself in the mean time?" You live life one moment at a time, appreciating yourself and the experiences that are in front of you. You make choices that are from love, love of yourself and love of God. It is not Source's desire for you to be unhappy and any situation that renders you unhappy has an alternative route available. I think that it is wise to use negative situations as directional signs to point you in the direction of where you need to be. Start looking at it that way and you will find your self less miserable when so-called bad things happen, but thankful for their role in your evolution.

I do know that it is difficult stepping out of your comfort zone, even when your zone is so very unpleasant. But realize that in some cases fear is a warning of the unknown, not necessarily danger. And when you are in situations that are not appealing to you, the unknown is perhaps just what you need to turn yourself around.

In Jacque's situation, she minimizes the power of the God within her because she doubts her ability to raise her children and create her amazing business. She will find that if she becomes in tune with her ability to do all those things with great success, the Universe will provide her with everything that she needs to be exactly what she wants to be. Then, because her husband is only reacting to her because of his own fears, his position will change or he will be removed from her life to make room for something better. It is amazing how, when we change, everything else will change to accommodate our success. Everyone is working through their own personal darkness and they are using us as we are using them: to help us discover our greatness by creating our darkness. We have to keep in mind that desire is of God. We are innately instilled with desires and talents that God knew would lead us back to our divine Source which is God. Our whole life experience was designed for that specific purpose, and this is how we know that we cannot fail. By releasing that thought we are able to more effortlessly continue on our journey. The advice that we give to others is the advice that our soul wants us to heed for ourselves. The practice of this advice will keep us in perfect peace and happiness and know that everything should be able to be exposed to the light. As a matter of fact, you want to expose it to the light because the things that are good when exposed to light will flourish and the things that are bad, when exposed to light, will die out. This is a win, win situation. Whenever you feel as though you have to keep something to yourself because of the repercussions it may have, know that this is and will be a stronghold for you, and therefore an area that requires your God attention and subsequent release. These types of situations will always be the indicator of the areas where you need to work and release yourself from shame, because there is nothing for you to be ashamed of. Do what feels right within yourself, regardless of how unsure your flesh may be, and your spirit will always keep you. Make your decisions based in love and love will reward and keep you, because love is God.

# 8. "If I like You I Must Screw You"

I didn't even know her name. The night we met we'd picked aliases and though we'd had relations on and off for the past nine months, we'd never divulged our real names. Sometimes she wanted some company, other times I did. Tonight I'd made the call. Superficial though it may have been, I wanted to feel a woman who I could connect with. I *needed* to feel a connection.

Maya and I met at our usual spot, Savoy. It was a discreet little hotel and I liked the set up—romantic with some special touches made with fetish buffs in mind. She pushed me down onto the bed, unbuckled my pants and reached into the flap of my black, silk boxers. Normally, that would have made me horny but tonight, I couldn't get into it. I lay there looking up at the ceiling, studying my reflection in the mirror above me.

*Come on, Mike, get into it. She's serving
her purpose.*

> *Yeah, but you know good and well this is not
> right. You deserve better than this. You
> know you want more than this so why are
> you settling?*

*Not settling just facing your reality. You're
just not meant to have a real relationship
with a woman. Besides sex with a near*

*stranger is better than no sex and no woman*
*in your life.*

> *Is it really? The fact that it's been five*
> *minutes solid and you're still flaccid*
> *says different.*

"What's the matter? You need one of those little blue pills or something?" Maya asked.

"I'm sorry. I'm just not in the mood tonight I guess," I replied apologetically.

"But you called me and...Marco (my alias) I'm horny now and I want...," she whined.

"Sorry Maya. A rain check?" I said, handing her a twenty for gas, followed by her purse and coat as I walked towards the door.

She snatched the items from me and stepped into the hall-way. "Only if you're lucky enough to catch me in the mood," she said indignantly.

I watched for a moment as she walked down the hallway. I closed the door then sprawled across the bed, starring back up at the mirror once again. I started thinking about everything that had happened earlier in the evening. I'd been out to my favorite supper club, the Chocolate Bar.

"...So what do you say, Keisha?"

"It's KaMeisha," she corrected me, fishing the cherry out of her drink.

"Pardon me. I was so taken with your beautiful lips that I...well there's no excuse. My apologies. What do you say KaMeisha?" I adjusted myself on the bar stool and gave her my best Denzel wink. "I'll take care of everything. Think you could handle that?"

"It's...interesting," she said, smiling slyly.

I was at my usual Saturday night haunt and by the time I met this woman, I was tired of trying to find a woman I'd actually want to get to know and just wanted some quality booty for the night. This one was younger than I usually went for; plus, I usually like a little more sustenance to a woman but her D cups and lack of a panty line, not even a sign of a thong strand on the hip, were reason enough for me to nix my 35 and up rule.

"It's an interesting proposition," she began. "I can see how that would be an impressive offer…to someone; but you know, I'm just not in the market for a Sugar Daddy right about now," she chuckled, her girlfriend echoing her laughter.

"Thanks for the drinks," they called out in unison as they disappeared into the crowd.

*Silly, gold-diggin', juvenile…women these days aren't 'bout noth'n. Don't know a good man when they meet one.*

"Ladies' man, Mike. How ya doin' tonight?"

I looked up to see Chico, one of the bartenders at the establishment, sliding a bowl of cashews out in front of me. "Chico my man. Been doing well. I just received word that my baby got a full ride to Stanford. Pour me another cognac, will you? Top shelf Hennessy. And a Cuban."

"Oh, yeah?" he said, turning to reach up and grab the bottle and an ashtray.

"Following in her father's footsteps, you know…"

"That's right?" he asked, sliding me my drink.

"…and business is good. I'm flying out to D.C. to close a multi-million dollar deal Monday."

"Sounds like life is good. So who's the lucky lady you're planning on celebrating with tonight?" he asked.

"There'll be a lady but she is not in here. Quality is next to nil tonight. The club's clientele is slipp…Aw hell no."

"What's up, Mike?"

"Veronica." I said, my eyes tracking her as she moved from the balcony VIP towards the bar.

"Veronica, Veronica. Which one is that?" He asked surveying the place.

"Light-skinned, shoulder-length curly-hair girl that Deja is serving." I couldn't stand the sight of her but for some reason I couldn't take my eyes off of her either. Never could I resist her…that damn charisma was what got me mixed up with her in the first place. She was the burgers and quiche type lady— one who could hang at the local dive diner and be just as comfortable at the most elite country club in town. Plus, she has a booty that won't quit.

"Yeah. I remember her. The lawyer, right?"

I downed my drink. "Mm-hmm. The one I was dealing with last year. Lawyer or not, that chick was just like all the rest. Thought she was going to play me."

"Naw, man. You said she was like no other. Had all her stuff together. Smart. Her own money. Sexy. No kids. You said she was the type that could keep your attention."

"Yeah, well…,"

"Matter-of-fact. That's the one you said had you thinkin' 'bout getting married again," he taunted tossing a handful of cashews into his mouth.

"I said wrong. She was a piece of work; one of those chicks that threw that 'I just want to be friends first' crap at you. I'm a grown man. I know bull when I hear it and that was that funky, rotten egg type crap right there. What 40-year old woman you know wants to be friends with a cat? What's the purpose? She has needs just like I do. We're two grown people. We can figure that friend thing out while we are getting busy."

"Alright. So if *you* cut her loose, why you acting all bent out a shape 'cause she showed up?"

"I told you. She's a gold digger. She wants and needs too much." *Man, she looks like she lost a couple pounds, firmed up a bit. Man Drain or not, she's still fine. What the hell is she doing with a sell-out like that? Is that an engagement ring? She didn't waste any time.* "Who's the Square she's with?"

"You know you not right," he chuckled, glancing down the bar. "That, my friend, is James Wilkes."

"Wilkes. Name sounds familiar. Can't be a regular. I don't recall seeing him here before." *He's a baby. Couldn't be more than 38. She couldn't control me so she went for a young buck that doesn't know any better. Bet she thinks she can train him. Stupid bastard.*

"As in *the* James Wilkes." He stopped pouring the Daquiri he was mixing and looked at me like I had a third eye on my chin, shook his head, then continued, "Owns Winstead Publishing. He's the cat..."

"Yeah well, looks like she has Urkel's nose wide open. Must of fell for that crap she was trying to shoot at me. Probably robbing him blind, giving him a passion play promissory note while they work on being *friends*."

"On the real, Mike, what's up with the chip?" he asked grabbing the Vermouth.

"No chip. She just pissed me off. Let me get another." I said sliding my glass across the bar. "See she got close. Closer than most, before I figured that out. I'm sayin' she was cooking for a brother. The home-style goods like Grandma makes. She'd give me massages. We did the poetry reading thing, plays, weekend trips, Jazz clubs, even had some good heart-to-hearts. I told her about my marriage, the ex-wife, my daughters. I was right for not totally opening up to her. I ain't no fool."

"What? She kept her dirt under wraps?" he asked, passing a dirty martini to the hand reaching out from behind me.

"Naw, she told me about her past boyfriends. Never been married...probably 'cause she's so frigid."

"Frigid?"

"Yeah. When I thought she was opening up to me, she told me about all the failed relationships she had and why she thought they failed and what she wanted her future ones to look like. Gave me some song and dance about that's why she hadn't dated much and had been celibate for the last two years. I'm a good guy so I listened. She ended the conversation saying she just wanted a friendly comfortable relationship, before she even considered sex."

"It happens," Chico interjected.

"Not in my world. In my world, I see a woman. She's attractive. I'm attractive. We're attracted. We do the do. We're done. Pour me another."

"It's like that, huh Mike?" he smiled, grabbing the cognac

"Just like that," I replied.

"And where did that get you? Here and alone, right? Maybe you should consider something new."

"Actually it got me *in* everywhere I wanted to go," I said reminiscing, "but since I'm not the type to kiss and tell, I can't share those stories with you."

"Aw, that's not right," Chico pleaded.

"But Veronica, she just didn't make sense to me. I mean, if you like a person, why wouldn't you want to be close to them sexually. Plus, I thought her spiel was her way of letting me know the goodies were ripe and ready for the taking. I mean it's the same tune all the women I've been with sang. But eventually, every freak showed out and gave it up. They all say they want intimacy with a man. What's more intimate than sex? Anyway, I kept seeing her. We were together for 2 1/2 months. Had a lot of fun but she wouldn't give it up. I figured if she wasn't undercover after sex, she was after my money, plotting or something so I starting do things to tick her off so that she would cut me loose."

"That's Veronica Pryor the Civil Rights attorney, right? From what I heard, that's not her sty…"

"One way or another she was trying to control me by not giving it up. I hate when women do that crap, trying to use sex as a weapon, or when they give it up, trying to control you by nagging you about what you promised you would do."

Chico shrugged his shoulders. "Maybe she was on the up and up."

"I'm telling you. A year from now you're going to read about Veronica and that wannabe Tiger Woods over there in the paper. She's going to stay with him long enough to divorce him and get half."

"And in your mind, there's no way she could have just wanted to get to know you 'cause you're a nice guy, regardless of your wealth power and career? All because she wasn't ready to have a sexual relationship with you? I mean, Wilkes doesn't have half the money you have, but she's with him."

"Hell no. Women don't operate like that. They always want something."

"Maybe she just wanted you."

"The chick is playing him, Chico, just like she was trying to play me," I said polishing off my third cognac of the night.

"I don't get you man. That Wilkes isn't any better than you. Matter-of-fact Mike, he's got everything you got…and what you used to have. So right about now, it looks like you played yourself on that one."

"Screw you Chico."

"No thanks. Got someone at home to do that. And you?"

I was angry when Chico said that to me. I guess because it hit home. As I lay there on the bed though, I realized that he was right. I didn't have anyone special to go home to and since I had dismissed Maya so abruptly tonight, it was doubtful I'd even have her pseudo-company to look forward to. *What makes it so bad is that I have no one to blame but myself.*

## Analysis

It has been said that "the enemy is really the inner me", and I wonder: if you were to be reflective of your life and personal situations, would you find this statement to be true? It is amazing how we can color a situation to fit our own need to support our fears. You have to look at your current situation and realize that if your current methods are not producing the results you desire, then there may be a flaw in the practice. You must also know that until you are able to address your personal issues and stop making justifications for them, they will taunt and haunt you until you do.

Mike is a man who achieved success in the eyes of the world; and yet, with everything that he has achieved, he finds himself feeling unrewarded in the way that appears to be most important to him. Yet, he is fighting with every fiber in his body to defend his current ineffective practices. Once again, the definition of insanity remains unchanged: it is doing the same thing over and over and expecting different results. We must get to the point in our lives where we are willing to stop defending antiquated practices and embrace new thought processes that actually make more logical sense. As I always say, if it does not make sense, then it is nonsense.

Everyone wants to be considered smart, and yet we tend to make fun of the smart kids and assign them names like nerds and squares. Why is that? Could jealousy of their talents play a part in our treatment of them? Look at the way that Mike put down Veronica's fiancé. Is it possible that he resented Veronica for having the strength to step away from old behavior patterns in an effort to expect and receive the rewards that she has so longed for?

People will tend to mock and belittle someone for not going along with them as they head down the familiar path of self destruction and disappointment. It sounds crazy but it happens all the time. If you look back in history, this is the practice of many cultures. We don't understand what it is that we teach and then we reprimand anyone that questions the very thing that we question in private. The truth is that we resent that person's courage and willingness to have understanding. We resent the fact that we followed blindly for years and we have an embedded need to hold on to our erroneous beliefs so that we don't have to admit to the possibility that we may have been wrong. The realization of this for most people seems to be intolerable.

The more beneficial plan would be to stop, regroup and embark on a more effective path, opting not to continue wasting valuable time. But the flesh/ego sports the cloak of false pride so well, and it has the ability to make a fool out of its willing subject.

Mike is drinking so much because he knows deep down that there has to be a better plan for his life. However, he finds the choice to "numb out" to the situation an easier way in the short term. But instead of him taking his life experiences and using them for what they were intended, as lessons to advance him on his journey, he will continue to fight until it starts to infect and contaminate every part of his existence. I think it is a positive thing to be stubborn sometimes, but it is a negative thing not to know what to be stubborn *about*. And Mike is being stubborn about things that are hurting him.

Everything that happens in your life happens for your benefit. Allow yourself to believe this and derive the lesson from every experience. Don't allow the opinions of others to confuse you and make you feel ashamed. Respect all the feelings that you have and know whatever you do should be done independent of the opinions of others and without regard to your fear. You can not fail, and only you can manifest your specific journey. Therefore, no one else can chart your course but you.

Mike pretended to open up completely to Veronica because he was afraid of being vulnerable, or of giving her ammunition that he believed she would be able to later use against him. But if he were to become of the mindset that no one can *really* hurt him unless he decides to feel hurt and that the pleasure of every experience should be derived at the time of the experience, he would find himself more open and at peace. The way to achieve this mindset is to become accepting of your life experiences and to forgive yourself for the very things that have made you who you are. We all must, independently of material things, realize our own personal value. Once we realize that material things are not indicative of whom we are, it enables us to understand that it is who we are on the inside which allows us to manifest our ultimate goals of personal fulfillment.

Another thing of which Mike is guilty, and a lot of us share this affliction, it is self-sabotage. When we feel ourselves getting close to the things that we desire, we sometimes find a way to destroy it by setting up roadblocks that we create ourselves (although we will often blame others). We self-sabotage out of fear of what life would really be like if we succeeded.

When you find yourself feeling shaky and insecure like this, address it with a frontal attack. Make note of when you feel the fear and then, at that very moment, ask yourself what brought it on. Ask yourself why you feel the way you do and what you think would settle your anxiety. This works, and it is a simple way to change your life.

There are three major components necessary for the success of this practice. You must be honest with yourself, you must be willing to do the things that you think would settle your anxiety, and your plan of action must come from a place of love rather than fear. For example, a fear-based action would be planning to see more than one partner, which will prove to lead you down your already destructive path. How will you know if the plan is love or fear based? You know within in yourself, but a helpful tip will be that love-motivated decisions don't create more drama in your life. They are usually the decisions that *alleviate* your anxiety, not those that create more of it!

Contrary to popular belief, *sex* is not the next viable step in a relationship after attraction. *Acquaintance* is. If as adults, we can show restraint and allow ourselves to get to know one another, allow ourselves time to understand why we are attracted to a person and why he or she has entered into our life, we will find life to be more fulfilling and a lot less complicated. Let "I like you" mean "I like you and enjoy your presence in my life and the gifts that you bring when I am in your presence", not "I like you and I want to rip your clothes off, so let's get busy". It is amazing that we have gotten to such a ridiculous place that we can say, "I don't know you well enough to open myself up to you in an intimate way, but I know you well enough to have sexual relations with you". Take the time to see the ignorance in this practice and understand why we are so ineffective when it comes to human relations.

With anything that you do in life, because everything is relative, decide what it is you want and create an effective plan by which to achieve it. Make sure that the plan you devise does not have negative repercussions and make sure that what you desire is what you desire, not what you were *told* that you should desire. And most importantly, allow yourself to see what it is you want without tainting it with the Hump Factor: "just because I like you, I should hump you".

# 9. You Owe Me

The alarm clock went off at 4:36 a.m. At 5:09, I hit snooze for the last time and dragged myself out of bed. Eyes still closed, I felt my way to the bathroom where I flicked on the light and turned on the cold water. I cupped my hands under the faucet and bent over so I could splash the cool water onto my face. As I stood up and opened my eyes for the first time, I looked into the mirror. I blinked as droplets of water dripped down into my eyes. I was exhausted; a fact that, looking at the mirror, was going to be tough to hide.

It had been a restless night, partly because I kept thinking about the local TV station coming to do a segment on my spas this morning and how big that could be for business; but mostly because of the drama I had last night with Kendra. I'm not going to lie. It shook me up. And it wasn't because I was afraid of losing her. It was because, for the first time in our relationship, I felt like I was losing myself. As I stared into the mirror, I couldn't help but think: How can a woman be good for me and *no* good for me, all at the same time?

Last night, Kendra and I had gone to a 100 Black Men gala—a five hundred dollar a plate dinner, to be exact—for which her company had purchased a table. The food was great and they had Floetry, Jill Scott, and John Legend as the entertainment so we jammed and danced for a while after dinner. Kendra and I hadn't danced like that since we first started going out. It was a nice, peaceful evening for us-until we returned from the dance floor, that is.

When we got back to the table, Kendra's colleagues were having a heated discussion on politics. They were speculating over who the candidates will be for the upcoming presidential election at first, but somehow the conversation turned to the fact that most at the table thought that "Republicans are running the country into the ground" as they said. Just as I was settling into my seat, the men at the table turned their attention to me and asked my opinion but before I could even form my mouth to respond, Kendra started chatting away.

"Oh yes, Honey. Tell us what you think," Kendra said, patting me on the hand. "Finances I can handle," she said turning to her colleagues, "but all that world affairs, political stuff, that's more Paul's forte. He's so well read. It seems like he knows a lot about everything. That's how he's been so successful. Like with his business. One of those books he's always reading helped him prepare so once we were able to secure the financing via one of my friends' investment connections, he was really ready to open up his first store and…"

"That was months ago," I interjected, smiling and putting my arm around Kendra. "The stores are up and running. All of you have been, right? Right? If not, you should really check it out. We've got the best masseurs in the Midwest and personal spa rooms for the soaks plus…"

"Oh, so they're fully operational?" Kendra's boss asked.

"Yes, why wouldn't they be?" I responded.

"I thought I remember Kendra saying something about you needing…,"

"Well you know how women are," I said nudging him playfully in his side with my elbow.

You are such a pompous ass. And you're not my boss. Why am I answering to you? You're no one to me, really. And I certainly shouldn't need to explain myself. So why they hell am I playing into all of this bull?

"They always want to feel useful or helpful…I think it's that maternal, nurturing thing…so I let her put in a call so she could feel involved in all that I was doing. I'm sure my sweetie felt a little neglected when I was preparing to open the first two stores, you know, so I was happy to let her have a little project. Got to keep the little lady happy or home goes to hell, right fellas?" I continued with a laugh. "But as far as the political question at hand, I don't know if you all are ready for my views."

"What's that supposed to mean? Are you a fascist?" Kendra's boss asked.

"Hardly. It's just…," I began.

"Don't be shy. We won't hold anything you say against Kendra…much," he replied with a chuckle.

"Actually, I don't think it's the Republicans that are messing up the country; neither are the Democrats," I said, choosing my words carefully to remain diplomatic. "It's all the greedy Americans doing a whole lot of whining about any and everything while doing a whole lot of nothing; them and folks who forget where they came from and only give back to our community when they get a plate of lobster tail, some champagne and a receipt in exchange for their 'donation' so they can have a nice tax write off come April 15th."

Everyone at the table went silent. I knew when I made the comment I would get a response. That was the whole purpose of me saying something in the first place; to let them know I wasn't some idiot just because I didn't have a MA or MBA from Wharton or Harvard or wherever they had theirs from. But I didn't know I'd leave them speechless. It was the company CEO, a well-groomed white haired man with a low afro who broke the silence.

"So I take it you're a Republican," he said.

"No," I replied, "just a self made American."

The man looked me square in the eye as if he was searching for something, then burst out with a boisterous belly laugh, "Youth. I love them! They speak with such reckless abandon;

without a care what others think," he finished, the others joining in on the laughter.

Did he just insult me? What? Is he saying I'm wrong or
don't know anything because I'm younger than him? He must
know I don't have my degree. These people are all the same,
trying to be all high and mighty because they have money.
Hell I'm just as good as them and one day, I will have more
money than they can imagine. "Glad you found me amusing,"
I said pushing back my chair and tossing my napkin on the
table as I stood up. I want them to know they don't intimidate
me. "Now if you'll excuse me, I need to use the facilities."

When I came out of the men's room, one of Kendra's colleagues who had been eyeing me the whole night engaged me
in conversation. She must have been new to the firm because I
had never seen her before. She was really cute and for the brief
conversation we had, she seemed quite intelligent. Even
though she kept the conversation friendly as opposed to flirty
I could still tell she was interested. Just as I was getting ready
to find out just how interested, Kendra walked up and stood at
my side without saying a word. She just stood there as if she
were waiting for me to introduce her. I wasn't about to do that
because then I would have had to attach some kind of title to
her. Realizing I wasn't going to introduce her, Kendra put on
her best fake smile, introduced herself to the woman, complete with her position with the company and assertion as my
girlfriend, then abruptly turned to me and said, "I was looking
for you." I didn't know what to do after that so I simply said,
"Well, you found me". Then, I shook the young lady's hand,
gave her my most endearing smile, and told her it was a pleasure to meet her.

As we walked away, Kendra flung her arm out sideways
clocking me in the chest with her arm. I looked down to see
our coats draped across it. "I take it that we're leaving," I said,
knowing it was a rhetorical question. She didn't even look my
way. Instead, she just handed me her coat, which I held for her

to put on, then walked towards the front entrance of the reception hall.

The valet brought her car around and handed me the keys. She stood, motionless until the valet opened her door. I got in, cranked up the car and turned on the radio. As we pulled out, she turned it off. She was silent for a solid ten minutes as we drove down Michigan Avenue. That meant that she was "composing" herself, which meant that she was extremely, not mildly but *extremely* "displeased", as she would say.

Kendra and I had been together for nine months and I knew the silence would lead to us arguing. I also knew it was an argument that she was not about to win because I wasn't worried about a little anger. I'd learned early on that with her I could win her forgiveness with the help of pricey gifts, pampering, and an apology consisting of a bunch of promises that I always meant, but never seemed to keep.

"I cleared my throat and reached over to stroke Kendra's cheek. "Come on, Sug, don't be mad. Whatever it is that I…,"

"You embarrassed me tonight Paul," she blurted out, ducking her face away from my hand.

"How did I embarrass you?"

"You cut me off when I was speaking and you acted as if I was one of your little groupies that you allow to help you with your career just to give me something to do," she snapped. "Oh, and I don't even want to get started with whatever the hell that was at the bathroom. You acted as if I didn't exist. You didn't even bother to introduce me to her and you let me stand there like and idiot. Why do I even believe any of the lies and promises that you make to me? If you don't want to be with me why don't you just let me know?"

"What? I didn't do anything!" I said, defending myself. Kendra just looked at me as if I had two heads, her eyes bulging out in disbelief.

"I did nothing but stroke your ego. It was mergers and hedge funds and real estate investments all night long.

Meanwhile, all I wanted to do was get you into the conversation so you wouldn't feel excluded. Then they finally talked about something and I thought you could contribute and you treat me like your flunky."

"Excuse me?" I said, trying to keep my calm exterior despite the anger growing inside.

"Paul, why do you insist on being so inconsiderate and self gratifying," she said sitting back in her seat. Shocked to silence I sat there trying to process the fact that she was saying all of that to me.

"What? I'm an imbecile now?"

"Unbelievable. It is like talking to the wall," she continued. "You act as though I'm the enemy. We are on the same team. I believe in you or I would not be backing you and supporting you the way I do."

"Oh. So I'm soft? Can't do anything on my own? Just an all out loser, huh? Why the heck are you with me then? The sex? Can't say I ever disappointed you in that area. Matter-of-fact, I helped you melt that frigid, Ice Queen exterior you used to have. I schooled you. You were the one who was limited until I came along. So now what?"

"So I'm so unsuccessful that I need you or I'm nothing..."

"You're taking it the wrong way," she said, rolling her eyes. "As I told them, you're quite well read. And I'd hardly call owning half a dozen spas across the state unsuccessful. It's just, well, on paper, you know you're not my financial or intellectual equal," she continued. "The truth is you're a thirty-five year old man struggling to make rent each month. I'm twenty-eight and make at least $50,000 more a year than your top salary at your last job and because of that, I am able to help you achieve your goals, but I want to be appreciated or a least acknowledged..."

"I may be struggling, but at least it's for something I believe in. My business. I see that as a worthy cause. What's your excuse Kendra?"

"See, why do you feel the need to go there. That is not even what I'm talking about. This is not about you being inadequate. This is about our relationship and how you treat me. I always have your back. Can you have mine? Plus, I don't need excuses. My life is just fine. Superb, actually. I have a great job. I'm on the fast track for advancement. I own a home. And I make enough money to keep you in the lifestyle you're accustomed to. So don't get nasty and hateful and envious because I've been smarter with my money, my life. And don't get mad when I remind you of it. Hell, you should want to keep up with me if for no other reason than to not hear me remind you of that fact. Or do you enjoy the feeling of being a 'kept man'?"

"I'm not a kept man. I take care of myself, my business."

"Really? Whose Jag are you driving? Who paid for "Les Miserables" and dinner last weekend? Who…"

"I could pay for those things if I wanted to go. And if we're talking truth tonight, I got your truth. Your truth is that you know that, deep down, behind that fur, the weave…"

"Why are you attacking me? I've done nothing but try to help you tonight, every night since I've known you and…"

"…and all that make up. You know you can't afford that lifestyle either," I continued, ignoring her. "Despite that front you put up I know you're struggling too. It's just harder to see 'cause when one credit card gets maxed out, you just move on to the next one and keep living the high life like it's what you're supposed to have, knowing your people are back home barely making ends meet."

As we pulled up to the stoplight, she opened the car door, unfastened her seatbelt and stuck her right leg out of the car.

"Turn the car off," she said through clenched teeth. "Get out my car. You're walking."

"What the he…," I began.

"You heard me. Get out."

Car horns began honking behind us. The light had changed and I could see headlights in the rearview mirror swerving out of the lane we were in to bypass us. "Kendra, I am not going to…"

"Just get the hell out. I am sick and tired of this sh*#$."

"Close the door Kendra. We're holding up traffic."

"Just get out."

"I will, once you stop acting like a crazy woman and close the door." Reluctantly, she closed the door. As I crossed the intersection, I turned the radio back on, tuning in to the Jazz station. I knew I needed to mellow out and I thought it'd help her to calm down too.

"Paul, I work hard and I am good to you," she said. I watched out the corner of my eye, waiting. I knew her and I knew she wasn't finished. She was processing. "As I was saying before that whole melodramatic scene you just put on…"

Can she go a sentence without insulting me?

"…I know you have challenges and issues and I accept that about you. That's why I'm here. That's why I've been here…to help you. Come on Paul, do you think I would've co-signed on a business loan or asked my friend to invest if I didn't think the spas would be a success one day? Of course not. Not if I didn't believe in you. I certainly…"

"Are you finished? I asked. "Cause we're almost to your house."

She glanced over at me then smiled. "Yes, I'm done."

"Well, all I have to say is whether you see it the same way or not, you punked me in front of your friends, putting my business out there in front of folks who probably already have a negative opinion of me and making them think that I need a woman to be successful."

"Well I…," she began.

"I'm not finished," I said, pulling up to my car, which was parked in her driveway. "What I was going to say was that I felt like you disrespected me. However, I can see your point and I appreciate your efforts tonight, but I'm a man. I can handle whoever, whatever, whenever on my own."

"Paul, it just seemed…," she started to interject again.

"Still talking," I said with a sigh. "You don't always have to have the last say."

"Sorry," she replied sheepishly.

"Forgiven," I continued. "And I guess I said what I said because it was just a reaction. I let my ego get the best of me and I went on the defensive. So, with that said. I apologize for embarrassing you, disappointing you, and anything else that I may have done tonight."

"Forgiven," she said, smiling at me for a moment, then flicking my ear lightly, "but only because you're so cute…and because you have so much potential."

After I got home, I kept thinking about Kendra and went to bed questioning the relationship. I'd considered leaving her but I'd been on a few dates in the last couple months and for some reason, I kept coming back to Kendra. The other women all seemed shallow. They didn't want to help a brother or have the patience to stick it out until I could wine and dine them the way they wanted. I guess that's why I've stayed with Kendra all this time. I do feel good, overall, when I'm with her. She does make me feel safe. Just not on nights like tonight, which seem, actually, to be most nights. When it comes down to it, I know Kendra only wants the best for me. And really, she is the perfect woman for the type of image I want to project and her social circle will prove to be quite beneficial for where I intend to go. Ahh! But is she worth it all? To stay or to leave? Who am I kidding? Stay, right? Then again, the cutie at the dinner might be worth looking into. You know, a little something on the side to let a man know that he's still got it.

## *Analysis*

Life owes you nothing. Does that statement surprise you? It's true and I'll say it again: life owes you *no-thing*. So when you do something, expecting something in return, you set yourself up for failure.

The successful way to approach life is to enjoy what you do because it is pleasurable for you, not because of what you might "get" out of it or what someone else might do for you. This way you are never disappointed and you are sure that your actions are not unconsciously done as an attempt to manipulate others.

Our basic conditioning has instilled in us the belief that whatever we have in life, we have earned it and somehow deserve it. This concept is false. Everything that you have in life was designed for you to acquire so that you can achieve your specific journey. Does this sound insane? Well, how many times have you said, or at least subscribed to the notion that what is for me is for *me*, and what life has for me I will not be able to avoid. Well, if you believe this, then why do you also believe you have to *make* things happen? A bit contradictory, huh?

Well, guess what: life does not need your help. It is not your *brawn* and brute force that brings your ideas into fruition. It is your *mind* that does. Oh yes, you have to act on what it is that you think, but it is really the thinking and believing that will make it happen.

People, and more commonly *women*, tend to gravitate toward projects. If you have a project to put all your effort and energy into, you feel "productive" and like you're making things happen. It gives you a false sense of control. Then, if your attempts fail, you can adopt the role of victim. "Oh, poor me, after all the time I put into that thing, look where it got me?"

Sometimes our "projects" are other people's "stuff". We get wrapped up in other people's problems and needs to the extent that we make a project out of it and take it on like a personal crusade…because we believe we'll be getting something out of it in the end. It is one thing to believe and support the efforts of others. It is quite another thing to offer your support to someone so that you can try to shape and form them into what you feel will be valuable to *you*. That's just plain ol' manipulation.

The healthier thing to do is invest your energies in *yourself*. When I suggest that you invest in yourself I don't mean to be *selfish*; I mean, spend your energy bringing about awareness of yourself and maladaptive practices. By doing this, you will attract to you someone equally yoked with you and facilitate the environment for success while minimizing resistance and strife. Adults can not raise other adults, so stop trying to "fix" and "save" people from themselves. And no one owes you anything for the choices that you make. We have to stop with these unwritten, hidden contracts that we make up in our own imaginations while forgetting the other person never agreed. We have to stop getting angry when our attempts to manipulate, control and trick people into doing what we want, fail. Do what you want because you want to and then you will find fewer occasions to feel resentful because someone else did not respond the way that you thought that they should.

When you try to orchestrate life the way that you think that it "should" be, more times than not, you are doing it from a place of fear, and fear-contaminated decisions create faith-contaminated results. When you desire something and then allow the Universe to reveal it to you then you will find success. But when you desire something and think that it is up to you to orchestrate how it will show up, what it will look like, and when it will be, you will find that the results will be less than favorable. The reason that you don't have the things that you currently desire is because you are not yet prepared for it. There is a natural process in everything that exists, and there are no short-cuts in this process because short-cuts delete steps and the necessary ingredients to completeness. Look back on your life: when times seemed to be the most trying, did you emerge on the other side a much more developed person for it?

When we elect to be around people whom we know are not equally yoked with us, it is because we like being in the position of having the upper hand. We want the other person to feel indebted to us because this gives us a false sense of pride and it feeds our egos. We hope that if the other person becomes comfortable with, or reliant upon what we have to offer them, they will think twice before wanting to leave the sphere of our influence. "Oh, but she NEEDS me; she'll never leave me now!" This behavior only demonstrates a poor self image on the part of both parties. When you feel that you are worthy of the best, you don't settle for less than the best.

The challenge with "training someone up" the way you want them to be, is that they are not sure who they really are and when they eventually find out who they are, no matter what role you have played in the process, that person may now have outgrown you and may need to part company with you in order to fulfill their life purpose. Ouch!

Life works in balance when we don't operate with hidden agendas. We have become so conditioned to working in the ego, using our sheer will to get what it is that we desire, that we have become accustomed to this system of passive aggressive manipulation to the point where it has created an illusion that we have bought into. We actually think that if someone has done something of value for you, you owe them something in return. No, you don't; and the way you can determine if the person was pure of heart when they did what they did is by observing their reaction to you. If they expect something in return, you know that they did what they did for you not out of the kindness of their heart but because they were trying to create a sense of indebtedness in you that they hope to cash in on later. "I'll scratch your back if you'll scratch mine." But a person who gave to you or did something to help you with no agenda will not give off the same energy of expectation. They won't expect you to "pay them back" for their kindness. Now, how many people do you know that operate in the later behavior? I'm sure the answer is very few. We have come to believe that the "give to receive" practice is the natural way because so many people operate in that fashion. But the truth of the matter is that just because it is commonly practiced does not make it in the order of God.

We have to retrain ourselves to give simply because it feels right and because we have something from which another person can benefit, and we need to be able to give without any expectations. This behavior puts us in line with the Christ consciousness that we so aspire to achieve. The easiest way to achieve this is to remember that you are intended to be an instrument of the Spirit and that your reward is in the proper functioning of this process. You can not be hurt by others unless you choose to perceive their actions as a personal attack against you, where you don't believe that God has your best interest in mind. You can't say that Source has you and wants the best for you and constantly consider yourself to be the victim. The two thought processes don't match. Release your so-called need to control, and allow the brilliance of God to express God's self in a magnificent way in your life. God is always present in your life; you just have to focus on His presence so that you are not so distracted by the imagination of your ego mind.

Another important thing to remember is that if you are ever on the receiving end of this "owe me" process as Paul was, don't try to use it to your benefit. This is the same ineffective process as the person trying to tally up the points. Sometimes because we want something so badly and don't have faith that

God will help us reach our goal we use the energies and efforts of others knowing that we will owe them in the end. How do we know that we will owe them? Because we feel the sense of indebtedness and we even say that we will owe that person. In other words, we sometimes talk ourselves into the indebtedness even if the other person isn't expecting it of us! We are familiar with the process and have seen it in action enough that it is embedded in us. Even though this process has been adopted as protocol, it feels heavy and cumbersome because it is out of order; and the participants usually end up at odds at some point in their unwritten agreement. You don't have to take my word for these things: take a look over your life and the lives of others that you know, with this new perspective in mind, and draw your own conclusions.

I'll say it again: no one owes you anything. Life is for you to experience the joys of your divinity, an opportunity for you to exercise your spiritual magnificence. Allow life to happen *through* you and discontinue the thought process that it happens *because* of you. You don't have to manipulate and strategize for what you believe your end to be. Understand that having a vision and planning is totally different from manipulation and strategizing. Awake every morning knowing that every small step that you make towards your desire is the way to fulfill your specific purpose, and that that purpose will be fulfilled in right time. Take the pressure off and enjoy the journey. Time is not the enemy and it is on your side. Your life is unfolding exactly the way that it was intended. You are not changing God's mind with your actions. He already knows who you are and what He wants you to be. The other busy work that you are doing He uses to train you up. How many lessons you get depends on how long it takes you to finally get it, but never fear because Source knows that too and has included that factor in your design.

# 10. You're Doin' Way Too Much

"Here," Scott said shoving the white plastic bag at me.

"Could you have taken any longer?" I snapped. "Stress is the last thing I need now and you're stressin' me."

"I'm not in the mood," he replied.

"Well, this is not about you, now is it?" I opened up the bag and quickly glanced at the contents. "What is this?" I said, rolling my eyes. For someone who's pre-med, he is so incompetent. I pity his future patients. "This isn't what I asked for. I'm not…"

"Look, that one was on sale," he replied, already halfway down the hall. "Either use it or don't."

"Something as important, as life-changing as this, and you get me a generic? Shows how much you love me!" I shouted after him.

Sheesh. What's his problem? He's acting like I asked him for a kidney or something. Whatever, I don't have time for his funky attitude today anyway.

I kicked the door closed, set the bag on the counter in front of me and leaned in towards the mirror to practice my facial exercises like my acting teacher, Valerie, had told me to do. "You'll never be a great actress until you can not only make the sounds associated with certain emotions but master the facial expressions you put with them," she would say. I couldn't help but laugh to myself as I pictured her the last time she'd told me that. She was always dead serious, but since she singed her eyebrows off and had been wearing penciled in brows, lately she looked surprised as she said it.

Valerie understands me. She understands that I have to experience life to be able to present realistic portrayals. I wish my friends understood me like she does. And Scott, he knows me better than anyone. Didn't stop them all from jumping on the bandwagon. God was that awful...

"Hey guys, what's up? You guys miss me so much you're throwing me a welcome home party?...How sweet!"

"Eve it..."

"Hey Scott. Why the long face? Where's my car? You having it detailed? If so, I need it back by 10. The White party is tonight."

"No, I'm not having it detailed. Your car...," Scott began again.

"The trip was so much fun. Bet it'll lift your spirits," I said taking a seat on the floor. "I saw Morris Chestnut the day I got there! We were in the airport and he nearly knocked me over—I was in my traveling clothes, you know so no heels— and boom, I walked right into his chest. Well for me, it was more like his abdomen, which by the way, was s-o-l-i-d. Anyway, he apologized. I said something—what, I can't for the life of me remember—then walked away. I thought it was the sign of the start of a great trip; but when I got to the hotel, do you know they had cancelled my reservation? I was pissed, but I didn't let it spoil the weekend. I ended up going to a random, second rate motel a couple blocks away where I had to pay cash 'cause for some reason, my debit/credit card wasn't working anywhere in that darn city...By the way Scott, I charged a couple meals and some drinks on your card since I was strapped for cash, okay? Anyway, I was so glad I had paid for all my event tickets ahead of time rather than leaving the $2500 in the bank where I wouldn't have been able to access it and..."

"Eve, the car is gone," Scott said, raising his voice.

"What?"

"I sold it."

"Why? What the hell? You had no right t…"

"I had every right. Besides, I did it so you could have a house to come home to."

"I think you're being a little…," I stopped mid sentence as Scott flung an envelope at me. I opened up the letter inside and read "Foreclosure: Final Notice". "Well this must be some kind of mistake. I'll just call and…"

"I already did and it's not," he said folding his arms across his chest. I looked around and all my friends had this glum look on their faces. Candace was nearly in tears.

"What's wrong with you?" I asked her.

"I'm sad," she responded. "I'm sad because I miss my friend. The one who spent time with us, not running off to parties and trips with strangers and who knows what, without so much as a call to let someone know you're all right."

"Seriously, relax. I told ya'll I was going to All-Star weekend."

"You left a six second message on my voicemail at four in the morning!" Scott yelled.

"Whatever. I called," I said under my breath.

"You know what? This isn't even about you calling or not calling. It's more than that," he hissed through clenched teeth. "You are doing way too damn much these days and the fact is, we're the ones that, one way or another, are paying for it."

"Don't think just cause you went off and got some college you can speak to me any way you want. I'm still your big sister. If it weren't for me you wouldn't…"

"I wouldn't have gotten there. I know. But if it wasn't for you, I wouldn't have to miss out on going back there next semester either," he exploded.

"Calm it down Scott," Candace said stepping forward. She stood there with her hands on her hip and rolling her neck.

You've got to be kidding. I swear I buried my Mama 8 years ago.

"You need to wake up," she continued. "All this mess you're doing…I know you call it experiencing life for your craft, but come on…running off on a whim, skipping out on work, not paying attention to your bills and other responsibilities, it's taking a toll on all of us. Especially Scott. That notice he handed you. It was real. 100% legit and if it hadn't been for him, your stuff would be out on the street right now. He sold that car and emptied his savings to catch up your mortgage payments."

"I would've taken care of it. It's only because they keep messing up my check at work that I got behind in the first place. The money was there. Then after that, they started tacking on late fees and penalties and bank overdraw fees. I've filed a complaint but they haven't gotten back to me and I wasn't about to shell out money month after month on that and have them keep messing me up, saying I owed them money."

"But why not," Charles asked. "Why wouldn't you pay? If you had $2500 to spend on tickets alone for All-Star weekend, you obviously had the money. Plus, if I know you, and I do, I know you had the works—manicure/pedicure, facial, waxing, massage and no doubt a junior shopping spree—before you left."

"I had to get right for the events. Image is everything. My future husband could've…"

"And that's probably why you couldn't stay at the hotel you booked, Charles said smugly, his right eyebrow raised. "You probably drained your account doin' all that."

"My account should have been fine. I just got paid and…"

"Not if the money you got paid," Charles cut in, "went to pay back the cash advance you made a couple months back for that singles Mediterranean cruise you just had to go on."

"How did you know about that?"

you were counting on doesn't come and you end up leaving us in a bind."

"Well, ya'll know that I'll pay you back eventually," I reasoned.

"Yeah, that's how you are able to get it from us in the first place," Jayden replied. "But the question is *when* are you going to pay us back? The whole scenario makes everybody tense: you put pressure on yourself because you want to come through and can't, and we end up feeling pressure and disappointment because we want you to come through and you don't.

"Why are ya'll throwing that up in my face?" I said standing up once again, "What is this? A 'bash Eve for living her life the way she wants' non-party?" I asked reaching for Scott's car keys. "Well, I'm uninviting myself as the guest of honor. I'll make it easy for all of you. If you don't want to help me, don't. I don't need you. I'm outta here."

Damn it! I'm losing them. All my friends. I don't know why I keep messing up like this. Why can't I straighten my life out?

I walked out and left them all standing there. I have no clue what happened after I left; but it's been eight days and I haven't talked to a single one of them since with the exception of Scott. I had to call him the same day all that went down so he could pick me up and have his car towed to a gas station; it was nearly empty when I took it and since my debit card was still on the fritz, I didn't have any choice but to call him. We talked that night and hashed things out but things have still been strained between us to say the least.

"Eve!" Scott shouted through the door. "What's the word?"

Startled by the sound of the doorknob being jiggled and pounding on the door, I spun around from the mirror, knocking the plastic bag and its contents to the floor. I sat down on the edge of the tub then reached down to pick up the pregnancy test that had fallen out of the bag.

"Oh, you don't remember?" Charles began. "That was the day you cussed me out because I didn't have the money to loan you because I was still low on cash from the last trip we went on, though I'm sure you don't remember much of that either since you were boozed up half the time and spending the other half with random men you met on the beach instead of me, the one who was supposed to be your travel buddy," Charles finished, rolling his eyes and looking away.

"You didn't have to put my business out there like that, Charles."

"Child please, you put your business out there long before I said anything today," he replied.

"You little...Aw hell no!" I said standing up and taking off my earrings. "Take that back!" I screamed swinging at him. He leaned back, causing me to miss his cheek. Scott caught my hand on the down swing and twisted my arm, causing me to sink back down to the floor.

I looked at Scott, then the rest of my friends. "Is that what you all are here for? To tell me that I'm a crappy sister and friend. To make me feel like shit? Well forget it," I scoffed, snatching my hand away from Scott. "Newsflash: You all are some trifling frien...naw, I can't even say friends anymore 'cause friends wouldn't get in my tail over small, meaningless incidents or favors. Friends would be glad to help me out when I need something just like I do for them!"

"It's not that we don't want to help," Desiree began softly.

"It's that it's become obvious that us helping you every time you get yourself caught up in something—men, money, work, whatever—doesn't seem to really be helping you at all," Jayden chimed in. "You stay in the negative because you're always borrowing from us. You always have a good excuse and then you put the beg on us trying to get us to feel sorry for you. You are constantly making plans with our money; and then when it's time to pay back money to us, the money that

"What?" I said peeling open the box and pulling out the directions. "Come back to lecture me or something?"

"It's not like that," he answered, "and I don't lecture. I just ask questions and state opinions."

"Yeah well," I said hovering over the stick, "it doesn't feel that way. Feels like you've been judging me all the time. Like you got some secret standard that I've got to measure up to, only I don't even know what it is," I finished, placing the stick carefully on the counter.

"There's no standard except the norm. All I want is for you…"

"Aw, here we go again. I'm not doing this today," I said sitting back down on the tub. "Go away."

"Oh, right. I forgot. You don't need anybody's help. Fine. If you…," he began.

Bill collectors. Man trouble. Disloyal friends. I can handle that; but this, this could be something totally new and…what about the time? The money? The responsibility? Or the father? I haven't kept in touch with any of those guys from the cruise. Oh God!

"Wait, wait, wait! Scott, wait! I said hopping up and flinging open the door." He was standing there, hands in his pocket with his disappointed face on. God. Is that the only facial expression you know? "Come sit by me. I don't want to be alone right now," I said reaching out to him with one hand and wiping tears away with other.

"Dinner's on Eve. I gotta keep watch on that and…"

"Is it wrong for me to want my little brother, my only family, here with me at a time like this?" I asked. "Just stay with me for like five minutes. By then we'll know if…"

"Just come out and let me know when you know, 'kay?"

"But I…," I stopped as my cell phone went off and Coolio's old school joint, "Too Hot" began to play. Thank God! A distraction. Wonder if my connect got passes for the party. "Hey, Shay! What's the word?"

"Come on. Not tonight Eve," Scott said shaking his head slowly. "You just got back...from wherever you disappeared to this time...and I told your manager you'd be in tomorrow. And if you're pre..."

I put my hand up, waving Scott away. "Cool. So can I wear the blue peek-a-boo pumps? And the skirt? I said pushing past Scott. "Alright. I'm gonna grab a shirt and I'm on the way."

Man, I'll be glad to get out of the house. All this stress. I need a drink...and a man!

## Analysis

"Keep it moving" is not the best way to deal with the issues that concern you. Distractions are just that, but reality will catch up with you and when it does, everything that you thought you were avoiding will be there, only multiplied. Eve wants all the things that most of us do, but she is pursuing those things in a way that is self destructive. Life without balance creates imbalance, and imbalance depletes other areas of life and creates problems.

This type of behavior is self destructive, and the unwillingness to listen to others that are expressing concern and shining light on her ineffective behaviors shows Eve's attachment to her self destructive ways. "The truth will set you free but first it will piss you off." (Gloria Steinem) Eve demonstrates a lack of willingness to take responsibility for her life, and she insists on acting as though she is being victimized by her family and friends. By carrying on the way that she does, it is clear that she prefers the illusion she has created from the immediate gratification of her actions to the hard realities. She obviously has an unwillingness to address her innermost feelings, and she appears to resent the responsibilities that she has. Eve is a classic example of the coined phrase "You can run, but you can't hide"; when you are unwilling to confront your issues, they will plague you in spite of your denial.

There *are* no short cuts in life and the life that you live has been designed specifically for you, because Source knows that you could not experience your purpose any other way. Everything that you go through, you can handle, and the things that you despise about your life are blessings in disguise. Even though they look monumental to you, God knows that you can handle them and that you will come through victorious. What a vote of confidence and superior value God sees in you! The trick is for *you* to recognize and know this as well.

It is often our own perception that taints our view of our lives. We sometimes have a hard time seeing past the problems themselves. Instead of seeing the benefit of the process that our circumstance provides for us, we focus on our situation as being negative. From this viewpoint, most of us adopt "victim" thinking and become heavy, angry and embittered.

Many people in today's society suffer from depression. Depression is just pent-up anger and frustration. If you believed that the things that happened to you happened in order to *benefit* you, you would have nothing to be angry or frustrated about. We would view our current problems in a more positive light if we could simply change our perspective on why we go through certain difficulties in life; and if we would trust that God does indeed know what He/She is doing and therefore we can not fail because Source said so.

The frustration that we often feel is because we believe that *our* will is not being carried out in life. But the thing to understand is that your will is *not* the will that will ultimately benefit you unless it happens to align with Source. The desire that has been placed in you is of God and any plan of God will manifest itself regardless of your ego-driven rants. So sit back and relax and allow God to be God.

People often say that God helps those who help themselves. Who started this misconception? That's what I would like to know! Sure, God works *through* you in order for the ideas of your mind to be manifested, but the process works much like a master computer in a robot body. The spirit senses a feeling, a desire. The mind originates the thought and the body carries it out. This is when it works in perfection.

Now, what if it were possible for the body of the robot to decide that it wants to make moves without the orders of the master computer? Chaos and malfunctioning would ensue. This sounds a lot like our lives when they get chaotic and out of control. But when we decide to listen to our own internal navigational system—what some people call the "voice within"—we find that life flows effortlessly and a peace reigns that passes all understanding. It gives you confidence because you know that the right things are happening and that it is being done properly. If you have not experienced this, I suggest you try it. Life was not designed for struggle, but struggle will be your life if you choose to live out of order. The best advice to follow is to rest assured that *you can not fail*, that you are limitless, and that every desire that you have untainted by fear is of God.

No one is in a deficit, regardless of what they may believe. We all have exactly what we *need* at any given point in time. So, if you feel that you *want* more, then start *needing* more and you will *receive* more. Let me explain how this works. Whenever I want a new wardrobe, I start by cleaning out my closet and making space in my life for a new wardrobe, and guess what happens? I *get* a new wardrobe. No, not overnight, but it does indeed happen. And why do you think that is? It is because I have created a need (i.e. some empty space in my closet) and because the need is there, it is eventually filled. The Universe abhors a vacuum, so in order for something new to come into your life, you have to make room for it.

Men often say, "I have not settled down because I have not found the right woman". But the truth is, they have not settled down because they are with *too many* women and there is no true need or space for just one. You see, you're committed to the results that you have. When a man gets serious about settling down, that will become his mission and then the Universe will show up and bring a woman into his life because *that* will be what he is focused upon.

Remember ladies, for men it is all about the right *time*, the moment when they feel that it is time for them to settle down, and it may not even be with a soul mate. That is why when you see the first signs that he is not being what he presented himself to you to be, I suggest you pull up camp. You can't change anyone but yourself, and sticking around to try to win the points that you feel will make you the self appointed winner of the game won't work either. If he is meant for you, he will return to you if and when he is capable of being who he is meant to be for himself and someone else. If he does not return then you should be grateful that the universe removed him from your life. Then look for the lesson and the blessing in the experience and give thanks.

When women say that there is a shortage of men, it puzzles me. Why then, are there so many couples? Look around and ask yourself: if there is a shortage of men, why do other women have men? Now, I am not telling you to compare yourself to them because the truth of the situation is that you don't know the dynamics of another person's relationship, and some of those couples are in relationships that are not at all healthy. What I am suggesting is that you could be counted in the number with the "haves" as opposed to the "have-nots".

Now, a man, *any* man, is not a hard thing to find, but a *good* man that is suited for you is a different story. So, the key is to not allow a man that is *not* best suited for you to fill the space of the man that *is*. Don't settle—the way Eve is doing, having so many men in her life that she might be pregnant but not know who the father would be! A "good man" can't come into your life if your life is already filled up by some guy (or guys) you're just settling for! Instead, you can be single by choice rather than by force, and you can use your spare time to prepare yourself for the blessing that God has in store for you. You can't expect others to treat you better than you treat yourself. Don't let others tell you that you are crazy and picky and any other negative deterrent that they can saddle you with in an effort to keep you from following the desires of your heart. The person that God has for you is perfectly suited *for* you and will be comfortable with every aspect of you. God does not make junk nor does God make mistakes: You were created and designed in your way for God's plan.

Eve automatically rejected her friends' attempts at an intervention to help her realize the problems she was creating in her life. When your loved ones share their feelings with you in an attempt to guide you, I advise that you get still and focus on Source. You will be guided internally as to which of the words that they speak are coming from their personal fears and which words are really for your spiritual awakening. Arguing with yourself internally is definitely a warning that you are operating from a place of fear, and constant drama is a way that you have chosen to distract yourself from dealing with the issues that are concerning you. Because we all have God living within us, we know what we need to do at all times—we just have to acknowledge that presence and that knowing. The consequences of the decisions that you make are the tell-tale signs of whether or not you are headed in the direction where you really want to go.

If you find that your life is not going the way that you want, just stop and chart a course in the opposite direction. Read books that will help you to navigate this new direction. Find like-minded people to keep you company. Seek out activities that promote your new lease on life and most of all, do what you know will give you the results that you desire. Again, remember you are committed to the results that you have.

All of this restructuring of the mind starts with knowing who you are if you plan to be highly effective. You *are* the living God. The Source dwells within you or you would be unable to draw breath. The fact that God dwells within should be evidence of your worthiness and His grace. Use that as motivation as you proceed through your life. What greater way to be given the support of the Creator? He dwells within you because he loves you in spite of what you do, what you believe, and who you think you are. Believe it or not, the road less traveled *is* the less difficult one.

# 11. A Lot of Nothing is Better Than a Little Something

"It seems like we haven't lunched in forever, Tony. How about Tuesday?"

"Not good for me. Wednesday?"

"Wednesday's a no-go."

"Thursday then. I can do Thursday at 11:30a. How's that sound?"

"One o'clock would sound better."

"No can do. I have an appointment at 12:30p. Don't know how long that's going go. Dinner?"

"Oooo. You know, I've got my…"

"Sounds like a no."

"Yeah but there's still Friday. Friday I can be flexible. Name your time and I'll fit you in."

"I'm meeting hopping Friday and don't have a clue when I'll be able to catch a break for lunch, a snack or dinner."

"Well, don't worry about it. It was just an idea."

"Sure thing Tanya. Hey, you mind hanging up my tie?" I asked, "Since you're already in the closet and all."

My wife and I had both just gotten home, she from a late night business meeting and me from a late night meeting of my own. The negotiation you just witnessed was a weekly ritual between my wife and me. We always seemed to fall into a particular cadence when we discussed our non-materializing standing plan to spend time with one another at an event that had to do with something other than our 7-year old son, Jordan. It was so common for us that it was like a dance.

"You showering tonight?" I asked.

"Ahhh, yes. I think I will."

"Okay then. You take this one. I'm going to grab a shower in the guest bath."

"Okay."

I reached into the bathroom, grabbed my toiletry kit then headed down the hall. Man, Chelsea smelled good tonight. And the paraffin wax, it made her feet feel great on my back. I can still feel it now. Her arms cradling my head, her legs wrapped around me, and those soft feet moving gently back and forth on my legs and butt. As I stepped into the shower, I turned on the water and switched the showerhead so that the water misted on my face, just like it had earlier that night with Chelsea, and relived the encounter, courtesy of my right hand. After I was finished, I reached up to grab the soap but caught my reflection in the partially fogged up shaving mirror hanging from the showerhead. I felt exhilarated but as I glanced in the mirror, I saw a man I didn't really recognize anymore.

According to the rest of the world, "Tony and Tanya are the perfect pair". To our family and circle of friends, our wedding was perfect, our life was perfect, and we were perfect. I admit they were right initially. Our life together really was perfect back when we first got together. It was the spring of our 9th grade year, time for the Sadie Hawkins dance. That meant the girls had to ask the guys to go to the dance. I had been asked by a few girls—six actually, two of whom were varsity cheerleaders—but was convinced if I held out long enough Tanya would ask me. I was right. When we got to the dance, I broke out all of my best moves trying to see if she could keep up with me. See, my father always told me that if I could find a woman who I could dance with I'd have a partner for life. So we were doing our thing on the dance floor. Then Da Butt came on. That was my jam. So I was grooving, keeping it real smooth for the beginning parts of the song then the chorus came around:

...*Keep your backfield in motion, hey! Doin' da butt...sexy, sexy...*

Every time the chorus came around I'd go lower and lower. I had to know if she could keep up. We got to the very last one and both of us were nearly dragging our booties on the ground, hers backed up right to my crotch. I don't know when she fell in love with me, but I swear I fell in love that night.

We dated all throughout high school. When we graduated, we ended up at rival colleges but that didn't stop us from seeing one another. Everyone said we'd grow apart in college but they were wrong. Our relationship matured so much that I proposed to her during the Fall Fest at her school at the beginning of our senior year. We married that spring on the same day as the Sadie Hawkins dance where we had our first date. It was rough at first—not because of the relationship though. That was fine. We were struggling financially. Neither one of us had been lucky enough to have a job offer straight out of school so we ended up living on the last of our student loans for the first four months after we got married. Just as that was running out, I landed a decent substitute teaching job and Tanya took a job in Admissions at the university which allowed us to make do until we figured out another way to survive. With that, we had money coming in to pay bills but we were miserable, so after four years of just working jobs, we devised a five-year plan to get ourselves on our feet and to get our careers on track. We agreed to keep our jobs but Tanya also chose to go back to school—which was great because it put her student loans back in deferment—and I went on the hunt for an internship that worked with my teaching schedule. Year one and two of our five-year plan went like clockwork. Tanya's classes were going well, I was happy with what I'd accomplished at the architectural firm where I'd been working because after my internship ended, I was offered an apprenticeship; and despite our hectic schedules, Tanya's and my relationship was sizzling! Five months into year three though, it all went to hell.

Year three of our five-year plan was when we found out little Jordan was on the way. Reality kicked in hard and fast. I'd never let him know; but between you and me, he wasn't in Tanya's and my 5-year plan. He just wasn't. I didn't know much about babies but I knew they cost money and I also knew there was no way I was going to be able to wait things out and see if I would get hired on at the architectural firm where I was completing my last internship. Sure, Tanya could've quit school and worked, but she was just seven months out from finishing her Master's. Plus, we figured her working and going to school wouldn't be good on her or the baby, so it all fell to me. So, I did what any other man would do. I hit the streets, called in favors, and surfed the Internet until I finally found a job. Me being the "lucky" S.O.B that I am, I landed in Pharmaceutical Sales. Been doing it for eight years now. Day in and day out, peddling drugs to doctors and hospitals that then dole the drugs out to patients, half of whom go hungry trying to afford them. This is what my career has become.

It was never supposed to be this way though. It was only supposed to be temporary because the deal was that when Tanya finished school, she would get a job so that I could reconnect with the firm. Somehow though, mid job search, she was presented with an "opportunity she just had to seize" to take over a dance studio. She did. She took over the studio, its five students, and its $45,000 worth of debt which, of course was on top of the hospital bills we were still paying and the bills we had before Jordan. I know what you're thinking: How did I let her agree to take over the studio. Well, I didn't. She signed the papers and then told me what she'd done. So after that, there really wasn't anything that I could do but work. Now, don't get me wrong. Pharmaceutical sales has served its purpose and it's not a bad job. But the fact is, I sacrificed my dreams for Tanya and now, looking back, it wasn't even worth it. She was selfish and manipulative the way she did me, chasing her dreams at the expense of mine. I could have been working at one of the top architectural firms in town. I could have been designing houses, museums, theaters, mixed-use developments. Who knows what I could've accomplished. That's history though.

Anyway, after we had Jordan my life went out of control. Everything that came out of Tanya's mouth was about Jordan needing this or that or some comment that basically always translated to the fact that I wasn't doing anything right. And to add to my dissatisfaction, my perfectly petite wife ballooned up during her pregnancy and only partially deflated afterwards. I used to think to myself she'd be thin again if she lost weight every time she opened her mouth to nag me about something. Don't go assuming I'm a bad guy for thinking that. I was young and I'm just being honest that that's what I thought at the time. Bottom line: Things just weren't the same. I tried for three years to make things go back like they had been but it just didn't work.

Eventually I started working more to steer clear of Tanya. It seemed to work—too well, I guess, because I found myself developing a life outside of my marriage; one that I liked, preferred even. It started with me volunteering for out-of-town-training; then I joined the regional baseball team which led to me making friends with some coworkers, which led to me socializing with them. Somehow, our favorite spots to go to ended up being jazz clubs and singles lounges. I wasn't going to look for anything. After all, I was, am, a married man. But somehow, I made a female acquaintance or two each time I went out. At first, it was just flirting, talking game like I would see my coworkers do and it was fun because I had never done any of that with Tanya really. She was my first and last girlfriend. Well, eventually, I'd hang out with some of the women in smaller groups, then it was one on one, not dating per say but seeing one another. I never took anything that developed seriously though. The women and I just had a good time. That's pretty much how it's been for the past four years.

Tanya didn't seem to mind me going out or even being gone when I'd take my excursions but I always thought she had to know what was going on. She never said anything though. At first, I figured it was because she had the baby to keep her busy. Plus, when she wasn't busy with Jordan, she always had a trainer or teacher of some sort coming to the house or the studio—Jorge for yoga, Michael for weight training though he obviously wasn't too good at his job, and Baxter...I don't know what he did but he's one of the ones that's been her Wednesday since the baby. After a while though, I started to think things weren't so innocent. And now, I do have my suspicions on Baxter's purpose in her life...the others too for that matter...but I don't say anything 'cause just like I'm grown and do what I want, I figure so does she.

Anyway, I ended up meeting Chelsea last year. I had gone out on one of my excursions, checking out some of the new architecture in Charleston and there she was, sitting outside of Starbuck's. It's been a real learning experience being with her because the relationship is so different from the one that Tanya and I used to have and it's free of the juvenile game-playing I experienced with the women I met when I was first hanging out with my coworkers. I guess you could say it's a taste of a mature relationship. Plus, with Chelsea, I feel like who she is now is who she's going to be five years from now and for the rest of her life. That's another thing with Tanya. I know people change but I don't even recognize her sometimes. She's just not the woman who I fell in love with. The woman I fell in love with wanted both of us to be happy in life and for both of us to reach our goals, personally and professionally. Her look, her demeanor, her ideas on life, her goals, her loyalty, it's all changed.

I don't see Chelsea everyday but I do try to meet up with her as often as I can because despite myself, I have begun to care for her. Hell, I even crave her sometimes. Today was one of those days. But would I leave my wife for her? No way. It's not that serious between us. If I were to leave my wife it'd be for me, not a woman. I've done enough over the last couple years for others. If I were to leave Tanya, it would be so I can live my life the way I had planned. Maybe go ahead and move to New York and become an architect; live in the penthouse of one of the condominium complexes I design, maybe. I even have a buddy up there too, to help me. Thought about contacting him a couple times but the salty reality is I can't risk being saddled with having to pay a bulk of the debt Tanya and I have accrued, which is what would likely happen since I am the man in the marriage. I'm sure you'd agree, we always get the short end of the stick when it comes to divorces. She'd probably try to suck me dry 'cause I doubt she could afford to live with just her income. Then there's child support for whoever won the custody battle...and it would be a battle because I know Tanya would never give Jordan up and I for damn sure don't want to be one of those AWOL fathers...plus, I just really don't see the benefit in letting her go. Being married hasn't affected my social life; there hasn't been a shortage of women willing to deal with me yet and I don't anticipate that changing even after Chelsea tires of my situation and leave me. Mind you, Chelsea has never asked me to leave my wife but I know it must be gnawing at her deep down. She's almost thirty. Isn't that what most women around that age want? A husband? I'm bracing myself for her to ask; but I think she hasn't because she knows that even if I leave my wife, I wouldn't go back to being anybody's husband, at least not anytime soon.

Startled by the sound of Jordan's voice, I let go of the soap and watched it bank off the side of the tub before dropping to the floor. "Jordy, what are you doing up?" I asked peeking my head out from behind the shower curtain.

"The shadows keep dancing, Daddy. It's scary in my room," he whined, tearing up slightly.

"Come on Jordy. Remember you're a big boy now. Remember what I told you about how to make the shadows go away."

"Yes, but Daddy I…"

"Okay then. Go on back to your room and do as I told you. I'll be in to tuck you back in after I dry off, 'kay?"

Jordy turned and walked out of the bathroom dragging his Elmo behind him. It's amazing how much you can love someone sometimes. Or, how much the love you had for someone can change and how the transformation of that love can change you. I closed the curtain and bent down to pick up the soap. I stood up, wiping the water away that was running down my face, and found myself face to face with my own reflection once again. This was not the vision I had ten years ago. Far from it.

With my towel tied around my waist, I headed down the hallway to Jordy's room to tuck him in. He was fast asleep when I got there so I just pulled the covers up on him and tip-toed out. I went back into the bedroom, put my pajamas on then slipped into bed trying not to wake Tanya. I situated myself on my side of the bed then closed my eyes, ready for the dream world. It was the only place I was truly happy these days when I wasn't with Chelsea.

"So since this week is out, how 'bout we plan a date for next week?" Tanya squeaked out softly in the dark.

"I'm game for that."

"So I'll just check my calendar when I go in to work tomorrow."

"I'll do the same. I'm sure we can work something out."

"Of course. We'll get together. Next week, we'll do something."

"Of course."

## *Analysis*

Better the devil I know than the one that I don't. This has been the method of operation for most people. "My life is not turning out the way I thought it should." Maybe that is because your plan was too small and you have to be urged through discomfort to abandon such a mediocre vision in order to embrace the greatness that is intended for you.

From the time that we were born, we were trained up in the way that our caregivers thought would be most conducive for our development. By embracing *their* desires and abandoning our own, we tried to find a way to assimilate what we wanted for ourselves into what others thought success should be. We found this to be difficult and chances are, we did not have good role models who could demonstrate highly successful results for us. Instead, our caregivers passed on techniques and behaviors that they were not quite able to figure out themselves, with the hope that you would be more successful than they. They never imagined that the reason those techniques did not work for them was that the *process* does not work because we suffer from lack of self worth and poor self image. We never assumed that the flaw could be in the process. We just naturally assumed that it must be in *us*. After all, all these ideas and concepts have been passed down from generation to generation.

But the fact of the matter is that if you look back on previous generations, it would be difficult to find those who were able to get highly effective results from their theories and so-called truths. If you don't get the results from the formula that the formula claims it can produce, then it logically follows that the formula is flawed. When you find you are operating with a flawed formula, you have to decide if you prefer to continue doing something that creates ineffective results, or will you step out and seek the formula that will render you the results you desire?

Now, in this process of seeking successful results, be cautioned that misery likes company. People want to be happy, but they sometimes resent you if *you* are happy. You have seen this time and time again. Now the logical thing to do would be to follow in the steps of the person that is getting the results you desire. But others may not realize that this is an option; because they have been fighting to hold on to what is familiar. Even if it is ineffective, it may not even enter their minds that there *is* a better way. Follow your inner God and be true to yourself and your desires will be met and surpassed. Guaranteed.

Tony steals moments of pleasure with Chelsea because he does not believe that he deserves to be happy. If he did, he would make a plan and implement it as though he deserved it. When you find people creating situations such as this for themselves, it is because they are afraid to let go of the standard that the world says will create happiness, even though they may have found happiness outside of that so-called master plan. "If I let go of my current situation, I may regret it. I may have to start over. I may make a mess of what I do have that is good on the outside. My personal beliefs could not possibly be correct. Who am I in the scope of this? What could I know? Maybe other people know better." So they continue living under the strain of dissatisfaction and deceit which can only lead to more challenges: garbage in, garbage out.

Maybe it is that you need to let go of your current situation before that you can see an even better one. Maybe it is that you need to start over because now you have a new perspective and a new idea of what a more satisfying life is. Maybe you need to lose everything in order to make room for the abundance to come. I think however, that the issue here is an internal belief that you are not worthy of more than you have achieved at whatever point you are at, and this is the pinnacle of your existence. This is an erroneous belief that should be erased from your consciousness and never be allowed to enter again.

If you subscribe to the idea that the physical realm is a lab, an arena where you are constantly learning in order to get the knowledge and understanding necessary to produce a happier life with no limits on how happy you can become, then maybe you will stop settling and appreciate that every experience is one that has occurred in an effort to bless your life. Be grateful, not discouraged and angry. It is like looking a gift horse in the mouth. The experiences of your life are there for your benefit and are designed to make you better prepared for what is to come. You cannot make a mistake; you can just have experiences or lessons that are necessary for the evolution of you. See, the need to forgive yourself is unnecessary—it would be like forgiving yourself for going to school. That is ludicrous. Your life lessons are designed so that you get to know yourself and the things that you like and dislike; the things you enjoy and disdain; and the things that you desire and those for which you have no desire. The whole process is about the self discovery of *you*.

When you live life in duality, you rob yourself of the joys that wholeness has to offer. You know when you are leading this type of existence because you have to live a life of deceit and fear in order to maintain the lie, even if you start lying to yourself to perpetuate the bigger lie to others. The goal is to live a life of integrity, where the words that you say match up with the actions that you take in all areas of your life at all cost. But what I find happens is that people believe what they say in theory, but don't apply it in practice and then start blocking out the fact that they don't live it in certain areas of their life. But the truth of life is that all things are relative and principals should always work or they are not principals, just theories.

I think we know that the duality of the life that we lead is not conducive to our spiritual elevation, but we use the excuse of "being human" to soothe the fears we have of our own greatness. Release and emerge as your true self and the petty rewards of "being human" won't stand a chance compared to the blissful pleasures of spiritual gratification. The spirit is never-ending, and therefore the pleasures that it offers are eternal. The pleasures of the flesh are temporal and fade with time. It's like the person that claims to dislike something that he or she has never had. It begs the question: how do you even know?

# 12. If You Can't Beat 'Em, Join 'Em

The vibrations running up and down my spine and the sweat forming on my forehead. That's all I could think about when I first sank to the floor in my apartment, trying to catch my breath after barely escaping a run-in with my ex. Does this guy have radar or something? How does he always know when I'm headed home? This is the fourth time in two weeks.

"I saw your car outside. Hood's still warm. Open up. I know you're in there."

But as I sat there with my back to the door, Donnell pounding and yelling from the other side, I began to get angry. Damn it! What is wrong with folks these days? How blunt of a hint do I have to drop. Not interested anymore!

"You know this isn't right. The way you did things...you can't just do that to someone. Melanie! Open the door."

You've got some nerve to be standing out in the hallway making all that noise. I have neighbors for goodness sake.

"Okay. Okay. I'm sorry. I just...I'm sorry. I just though that we were...I guess it doesn't matter what I thought..."

I mean really. All that "I thought we had this. I thought we had that". Whatever. Obviously I disagreed. So why are you here?

"...But still, the least you can do is talk to me, woman! Melanie, please."

"What have you gotten yourself into girl?" I whispered to myself as I caught a glimpse of my reflection in the cabinet beside me. I sat there, studying my reflection and listening to Donnell's pleas. "This is exactly why you should've let him go when you got that first 'I was just thinking about you' call." I've been through this enough times—on both sides of the situation. I should've seen the signs. All the times I've been the one in relationships doing the same thing…but not anymore. I'm not that woman anymore. That's why I dropped him. That's why he's out there whining like a little girl and I'm in here.

I remember the day that things first started to change for me. It was seventeen days after the break-up with my boyfriend of two and a half years, Sean. I loved that man. He loved me too, I'm pretty sure, but he wasn't in love with me. You know there's a difference, right? I didn't then but I'm well aware of that fact now. Well anyway, I did any and every thing I could for that man to keep him happy. I supported him through all of his important trips and meetings and outings and cancelled dates—all of it. We talked about taking our relationship to the next level but that's all it was, talk. After all that talk, he dumped me, claiming he just wasn't ready for a serious relationship. At the time, I was stunned and heartbroken so I said nothing. I just cried as I watched him walk out of the door.

I hadn't moved an inch when my mother walked in the house two hours later. She turned on the lamp, grabbed my chin and lifted it to look in my red, puffy eyes then looked me dead in the face. "You did this to yourself," she said. "You gave him too much of you. He didn't deserve it. Don't ever let a man do that to you again. Adopt the man's mentality on life and love and you'll see that you are the one in control of your life, your happiness, and how you are treated in your relationships." She was so harsh with her words that night I didn't know what to think. But something did click in my mind because before she left the room, my tears had dried.

I woke up the next morning feeling like I had never felt after a break-up. I was refreshed and optimistic. I even left the dull, dark clothes in the back of the closet and shifted my sexy active wear to the front. Determined to move on with my life, I headed to work with my head high. I walked in to the gym to find that all the classes I was slated to teach that day were filled and that my report from my supervisor was good enough to put me in the running for a raise. It was a great day and I knew it was all because of my newfound mindset on life and love.

I admit it was a few weeks before I stepped back out into the dating arena, but when I did, I was ready and I was in control. I did everything I had been too afraid to do before. If I saw a man I liked, I approached him or gave him my business card. If a man I felt was nothing but talk and game stepped to me, I dismissed him without hesitation; before, I would have entertained him to protect his ego but not anymore. The men I'd dated hadn't ever worried about my ego or feelings so I figured, why should I? Before I knew it, I was dating three different guys at the same time and a few stragglers in between. It was wild because I had always thought of myself as a one-man woman, but I liked dating multiple men. I mean, I really liked it because I could get all the things I was looking for in a man at the same time—just through three different men—and when I tired of one, I called another. I was the one in control of the relationship, deciding how much of me a man got to know. Finally, I was the one who was getting my needs met without having to give up too much. What I liked most though, was the power that I felt. I was calling the shots and I didn't care about pleasing some man. I dressed how I wanted. I said what I wanted and I did what I wanted. All that gotta do this and that to keep a man, that B.S. went down the drain with that last relationship. Why? Because I wasn't worried about being alone, or losing the men to some other woman.

Why would I be? I had plenty of men, all of who were with me on my terms. If they didn't like how things were or what I did, they were free to go. They knew from jump I was not and would not be pressed over them. Dating like a man has been a for real an eye-opening experience.

There are three guys I'm dealing with—Donnell out there, was the fourth, but you see how he's acting. He's too emotional. Too needy, thinking I wanted to be with him every moment of the day, and too naïve thinking that he could mold me into the woman he wanted if he just waited around long enough. That one backfired on you big time, didn't it fella?

I met all of the men in different places, but I guess I took to Donnell so much because unlike the others, I wasn't on the prowl when we met. It was three months or so ago. I was dressed in my favorite jersey, high on Funnel Cake that had been drenched with fruit and confectioner's sugar, and shouting the most un-lady like things I could think of at the umpire. I caught a glimpse of Donnell when we were both diving for the baseball headed straight for our section of the stands. He said, "Excuse me, Miss," which surprised me because I hadn't met a man with manners like that since my father. Then, he literally snatched the ball right from under me. I was heated. I had plans for that ball! Still, he had managed to arouse my interests, so the next inning, I bought him a beer. Soon after, we got to talking and from there it was on. We became baseball buddies, then booty buddies. He was still dating other women—at least I expected that he was—and he knew I was dating other men because that's something that I always put out there from jump, so it was all great for the first couple weeks. But last month, he started trying to see me every other day and monopolizing my weekends...and got upset when I didn't drop all my other plans for him. I guess it was his not so subtle way of saying he was interested in a committed relationship. I liked spending time with the cat but that's not how I operate, 'cause I know from experience if you give them your time, your heart almost always follows; and when men get your heart they don't know what the hell to do with it. I'm not up for that these days. After a few weeks, I suppose he got frustrated and that's when he came at me direct, asking for a monogamous relationship. I'm not going to lie. I considered it for a second. After all, he was a pretty decent guy; one of the few I had met in a while who was almost completely the man I was looking for; but then I remembered I'd thought the same about my ex, Sean, and that thought was dropped from my memory with the quickness. Still, I am going to miss him because out of my current beaus he was a good guy to chat with. A listener, you know, and he would do this thing with his ton...that's beside the point. I'll miss him but he had to go. The others, while they have their good points, listening just isn't one of them. Now, they're all fine—that's a fundamental requirement—but outside of that, they're a mixture of a whole lot of man. Before, I never knew what I was missing out on by limiting myself to a specific type of man. I used to have strict guidelines: African American, heterosexual, college-educated, age 28-32, 6' or taller, making at least $65,000 a year. Now, the height requirement still stands and he's got to have at least one tasty feature to his physique. But for the most part, he just has to be good looking and able to meet my needs, whatever they may be at the moment.

Anaccio is my young buck. He's a high-energy import from Greece and it's always an adventure with him. What he's lacking in maturity, he makes up in creativity. The things that man comes up with for us to do! He's my fun guy. Then there's Lawrence. He's a good old-fashioned down home, blue-collar man. With him, what you see is what you get. Nice build, a little undercover thug in him. Meanwhile Jamison, an uncommon mixture of Japanese and American Indian, is my go-to guy when I want to experience the high life—limos, five-star restaurant dinners, and cultured events like the opera. And of course when it comes to bedroom, all of them put it down in their own unique way. Yummy. So what's in it for all of them? No hassles. They know if we jive, we jive; if not, I won't be running after them begging, creating scenes and what not. I don't have time for that. Besides, I refuse to lose my dignity to a man again. If they don't like the way I do things or the fact that they're not my one and only, they've got to go...and in Donnell's case, his time was just up. When they try to make me into a one-man woman, that's always when they have to go. And if I see him out with another girl, he's got to go too. That's not cool. It's disrespectful and it makes me look like Boo-Boo the Fool and I'm not having it. So when that happens, it's over. That's the trouble I come up against sometimes though. Just when I assemble the perfect "man" one of them starts to slack up in their "designated area of expertise", or he just dissatisfies me in general and I have to go through finding a replacement. Somehow the jokers never see it coming. I don't know how they miss the signs 'cause I know they've done it to women before...Hell, I know that from firsthand experience. And just to be clear, I don't take pleasure in letting them go...not much at least...but it is funny because it seems like as soon as a man gets a taste of what he's probably been doing to women for years he crumbles and pouts like a little child who has just had his Popsicle snatched. It's a sorry sight to see a grown man whining like ol' whining Donnell out there but hey, this is how the dating game is played these days. Momma was right. There is something empowering about dating like men do.

"Mel, if you would just give us a chance..."

I stood up and peeked through the peephole. I could see Donnell leaning against the wall, his left hand above his bowed head. Trouble is, I'm not a man. Sometimes I...

"Melanie? Baby? Just..."

Is he crying? Oh hell, no! I can't listen to this all night. I reached in my purse and pulled out my cell phone. I got up from the floor as the phone was dialing and walked into the kitchen to grab some water.

"Melanie?" I heard him answer outside the door.

"Hey Donnell," I replied.

"I've been trying to catch up with you," he blurted out.

"So I hear. My neighbor called. Said some guy was outside of my apartment banging on my door. Figured it was you."

"Yeah. Well, I…"

"I'm downtown right now. Why don't you go to the diner on 8$^{th}$…"

"Really? I'm there!" he said hanging up the phone.

"I was hoping you would be," I said aloud to myself after hanging up the call. But I never said I would be. Man, this has just gotten way too easy.

## *Analysis*

Why do you think that by becoming the very thing you dislike, you will be satisfied with your life? Ultimately, everyone desires the same thing—to be treated decently and with respect—and when mistreated people will respond the same way regardless of gender. Melanie believes it is perfectly fine to treat Donnell badly (and to use a string of other men as well) because that's how other men have treated her in the past. She felt like a victim after Sean left her, and she made a decision she would never be a victim again. That in itself is fine, but it's how she is going about *implementing* that decision that is creating problems in her life. She doesn't see that her "an eye for an eye" approach is not only cruel (to Donnell, in this case) but is also not getting her what she really wants: one good man to love her and treat her well. Instead, her ineffective choices are only giving her *partial* satisfaction on a short-term basis, because her ego is calling the shots. She doesn't *think* she's settling—she thinks she's totally in control—because her ego is rationalizing her behavior. But as we know, the ego is not interested in lasting results because the ego itself is temporary. When someone is more concerned about immediate gratification, they are really running from their innermost desires because of the fear that those desires will never be fulfilled.

If we get out of the role of victim, it gives us an opportunity to view the situation from a place of confidence and that place allows you to be more discerning in your choices of whom you allow in your space. Remember that everyone is trying to get his or her needs met. Some will get their needs met pleasantly and diplomatically, while others will be more inconsiderate and ruthless. When someone does something to you that you do not like, that person has usually convinced himself or herself that their behavior is perfectly justified (at least, from their point of view), so the sincerity of their conviction is strong.

But the responsibility for *your* reactions and choices is *yours*. No matter what someone else says or does to you, you and you alone are responsible for what you want to do about it. You can take the "an eye for an eye" approach—like Melanie, which rarely works that well—or you could try another approach, one that will get you much better results in the long run.

If you look at the situation with an objective spirit, you will find that in most difficult relationships, both parties had hidden agendas and were implementing ineffective behaviors to achieve their desired results. But it is usually the one that did not get the upper hand that cries "Victim!" the loudest. The truth of the matter is that *both* parties are losers in the situation because the one that appears to be the victor is also disappointed. He or she was convinced that *this* time it would be different, and then found out in fact, that it was not. Sometimes, when you think you're "winning" one thing, you're really losing something even greater. That realization brings sadness and disappointment, the ceremonial robe of the victim. You see, the major missing awareness in this situation is this: it is not the *situation* that changes a person; it is the *person* that changes the situation.

Everyone wants something beautiful and magical in their lives especially when it comes to a life partner. There's nothing wrong with this, unless our major reason for wanting a life partner is because we want to push off the responsibility for our happiness onto someone else. In other words, we think our only path to happiness is through that life partner. This path seems overwhelming, so we want a magical solution to the challenge in the form of the "perfect" partner who will come along and bring us everything we think is missing from our lives.

But we often want things that we are not prepared to handle. Children want to be adults, workers want to be the boss, players want to be the main object of desire, poor folk want to be wealthy, students want to be teachers, and humans love to play God the Father. When you understand that life happens in process and that everyone is in their own process, there is a certain level of maturity that accompanies this understanding.

Everything we achieve is process-involved. There was a process that produced you and evolved you into who you are. From conception to birth, from baby to toddler, from toddler to child, from child to adult, and from human awareness to spiritual awareness, *process* is the design. Life demonstrates for us the formula for transformation and evolution of self. God is all knowing, so my money is riding on the fact that this is how life must work to facilitate successful progress.

Therefore, it naturally follows that if a person is not where we would like him or her to be, it is because he or she is "in process"; and we will not be able to speed that process up, especially not for our own benefit, because the process is not about *you* it is about the other person being in process. And what happens during gestation when the process is interrupted? The baby may or may not be born, or if born prematurely, there can be defects.

Learn to spot someone who is in process and is not at the same level of awareness as you are. You will find that this will minimize many conflicts in your relationships. This is why it is so important for people to be equally yoked. If you are both at the same level of awareness, then each will understand the plight of the other and will be able to offer support through the process—not one person waiting on the other to "get it". If you are unable to live with someone else's negative behaviors, then walk away. A person could have a million good points and one bad point that outweighs all the good, and that's going to be the "deal-breaker".

Giving more in order to *get* more will not work either. If you are giving more of yourself with the expectation that the other person "should" be able to give more to you in return, you're likely to be disappointed, because people can only give what they have to give. People may *want* to change or may *want* to give, but they have not yet built up the foundation within themselves to be able to deliver the results they want, and they need to continue on with their process in order to be able to do that.

Sometimes when we are in relationship with another, we are not necessarily going to be rewarded with that person's presence for a lifetime. Instead, it is possible that we are the *instrument* that Source uses to help guide that other person through the journey to his end result. Boy, we don't like to hear *that*, because we want what we want—especially when it comes to relationships, huh? Life is not about the achievements of your flesh; your flesh does not understand that its role is that of servant, not master. The desires of the ego are irrelevant, and when you place the desires of your ego high on your priority list, you are bound to be disappointed.

Life will reveal and present to you the best things for you, and when you receive them you will find that they will surpass your wildest dreams. It is natural to have the desire to share your life with another. The desire is of spirit; the anxiousness to achieve it and the frustration you feel because you don't have it right now, and the fear you experience because you think it may not exist or come, is all a part of the flesh, and the devil is a liar.

Melanie is acting from a place of fear, and she is behaving the way the stereotypical man conducts himself—jumping from one partner to another while never letting herself get too close, all under the guise of being the one who is "in control". She is getting the same results from having all those different men in her life that non-monogamous men derive from playing the same games with many women. Flesh games are very emotional, because when the players don't get their desired results they have temper tantrums and often throw caution to the wind in order to feed their ego cravings. The end result is that they never achieve their real goals.

People often think that it is easier to stay in an unsatisfactory relationship than to leave, but I beg to differ. When a person takes the step to move on, it actually takes less effort than it does to stay. It is like moving a bolder up a hill when you make the decision to stay in an ineffective relationship. But when you decide to leave a situation that strains you emotionally, it is like pushing a bolder *down* the hill. Which do you think is easier to do?

Stop the unproductive cycle that has not produced the results that you so crave. Let people be who they are right now, and stop putting pressure on them to be who you *think* they should be because it suits your needs. Believe it or not, everyone is doing the best that they can and if their current best does not meet you expectations, then bless them and release them. If a person is meant for you, he or she will return to you—but in a way that will be beneficial for both of you.

When you meet someone for the first time, the dynamics of that first encounter are often misleading. It is like you are viewing your new prospect while under the influence, where your "drugs of choice" are possibility, lust, anticipation, hope, and fascination. It's like drinking a potent 200-proof cocktail that creates an intoxicating haze and renders you incapable of making the best decisions for the next phase of your life. You can not control the actions of another, so if your new prospect's intentions are to deceive you, there is nothing that you can do about that; but if you allow the fog of the euphoric "love cocktail" to lift, it will give you some space to see things more clearly and to make healthier decisions. We have been conditioned to "go for it" and afterwards discover what it is that the situation can offer us. This has proven to be a highly ineffective plan.

So let's try something a little different, something that at least offers the possibility of success. If the person you are with is unable to allow your relationship to unfold and present itself *slowly*, then he or she is not the one for you. Why? Because they may have the same intentions and desires that you do, but they may be working with old behavior patterns and expecting new results, and this won't work. Actions must line up with intentions to produce desired results. You should be able to cover your ears and look with your eyes to see if the person is who they say they are, because actions are the true manifestation of who someone is.

Instead of being heartbroken or disappointed when someone turns out not to be the person you thought he or she was going to be, be thankful that you were able to discern it. This actually means that you are becoming more observant about what works or doesn't work for you, that you are reacquainting yourself with your internal navigational system and that you are getting closer to your goal because you are not settling for less than your desired end. Also be happy for the other person because he or she is coming closer to his or her own goal. By you *not* indulging their ineffective behavior they may become more aware of useless practices; and whether they acknowledge it at that very moment or if it hits them later, they have been encoded with information that will help them in the future.

Don't deny your desires; allow yourself to feel and experience the joys of life, but never settle in the process. If you can conceive it, then obviously it exists, but as long as you fill the space with what you don't want, you can't receive what it is you *do* want. God supplies needs, but the need must be there to be filled.

# 13. You're Doin' the Same Damn Thing

"Our next caller is Michelle out of the Georgetown area. Michelle, what's on your mind?"

"Hey Dr. Diante. I have a comment, more than a question," the woman replied.

"Go ahead," Diante replied.

"Men need to stop lying!" she screamed. "It's immoral and the women they're dealing with don't deserve it. You hear me?"

I looked through the glass into the DJ booth, my eyes popping out with surprise. Diante was on the verge of cracking up on the air. This woman has got to be crazy. It wouldn't be a Friday show without at least one crazy female caller. I started twirling my right hand index finger in the air signaling him to wrap up the caller. He held his hand in the air acknowledging the signal I'd given then leaned into the microphone. "Whoa! Whoa! Whoa!" he said regaining his composure. "That's a loaded statement. What are men allegedly lying to these women about?"

"Everything. But mostly about wanting to be in a relationship. They say all the right things to keep you close and get you hooked; then when it comes time to step up to the plate and take things to the next level, bam! Things start falling apart," she shouted hysterically.

*Sounds like she's been reading a page out of my diary. Tell it girl. Men do do that crap.*

"...Ignorant," she continued.

"Thanks Michelle," Diante said, clipping the call and signaling for the closing music for the show, "but you have to take some responsibility for the relationship too," Diante replied, taking a long pause and peering through the glass.

*Why is he staring at me like that? How could he possibly...he couldn't. I don't even talk to anyone up in here.*

"...If you can see now that the men didn't want to be in a relationship," he continued, "what was keeping you from seeing it when you were still dealing with them?"

*How can you say that? She probably had no clue that those men were playing her. I didn't know what Justin was up to when we were dating, that's for sure.* I began waving my hand giving the wrap symbol more ferociously. Diante, you're going too far with this caller.

Diante didn't bat an eye. He maintained his gaze, a slow grin crossing his face as he continued speaking his mind.

"...Or was it that you just didn't want to see?" Diante continued without batting an eye. He maintained his gaze, a slow grin crossing his face as he continued speaking his mind. "Can't say nothin' when the truth is spoken, can you? Get a grip Mad Michelle. Ponder that one folks. This is Dr. Diante for Talk Radio 970 AM, WLKP."

Just as we went to commercial, Diante stood up, and winked at me while gesturing as if he were shooting a gun at me. *I hate you. I hate you. I hate you. You're a freaking prick!* Diante left his booth and I immediately stood up, gathering my things so I could get out of the office fast. Diante had been drinking water the whole show so I was banking on being able to get past him at the very least. No such luck.

"Pretty good show today, huh Sasha?" Diante asked, peeking his head into the producer's booth. I didn't like his smile at that moment. It was one of those 'I know something you probably wish I didn't know smiles'. *But then again, he kind of always looks like that. But no, he looks extra devious today. He knows something about me or he wouldn't be standing there like that. But how? How the hell could you possibly know about Justin? Oooo, I bet it was the busybody in Traffic, Angela. She must have been listening in on a conversation I had with Reggie B. or one of my other friends. Is there no freakin' privacy or semblance of respect at this radio station?*

"Yeah, I bet you loved every moment of it, especially that last bit." I replied picking up my shoulder sack and coffee mug. "Did that get your rocks off?" Oops. *Did I say that aloud? I've got to get out of here before I say something that'll really get me fired.*

"Actually, my rocks are quite settled," he said with a slight laugh. "What the hell are you talking about?"

"Come on Diante. You may be a smart psychologist but you stink at playing dumb," I said rolling my eyes and pushing past him. *What a jerk!*

Not wanting to get caught in an elevator with anyone from my office, I decided to take the twelve flights of stairs down to ground level. As I stepped outside, it started raining. I didn't have an umbrella on me. *Perfect end to a perfect day.* So I pulled my coat around me, tucking my backpack tight under my arm then sprinted to the King Street rail station. As I entered the station I saw that the train doors were just about to close. "Please! Wait!" I yelled. The doors stopped moving. I looked down the train and saw the conductor peeking out. "Thanks," I yelled, stepping into the car. *So you haven't forsaken me. Thank you Lord!* I plopped down on the first seat I could find; a window seat next to an old man who smelled of old urine. *Or maybe you have.* I sat there with my back to the man and my hand covering my nose and mouth, trying to shield my senses from the scent. *Just four stops 'til I meet up with Reggie B. I'll be there in no time.* As the train took off, my thoughts wandered from the foul smell back to my office trauma.

*It had to be Angela running her mouth. That's got to be how he knew. Then I bet she told Lyssa who's shackin' with Joseph, who brown-noses Carter, which, is probably how Diante found out. Great. And now I'm going to be the talk of not only the station but the entire town. Damn it! Wonder how long that's going to take to blow over? Maybe I'm overreacting. Am I? Maybe. Yeah, maybe I'm just being hypersensitive 'cause of what Reggie B. said last night. I guess there may have been an itty bitty bit of truth to what he had to say.* Lost in thought, I watched the city scenery fly by—cars, people, and buildings—and even though I'd taken this route many times before, I was startled when the scenery blacked out and my view became my own reflection. Though I remained steady, I noticed that if I focused on where my reflection was I could always see it, no matter what background flew by, and that if I didn't focus on the spot where my reflection was, it kept fading in and out as the background behind it changed. *Funny. That's just what Reggie B. said earlier this week.*

"All right. So go ahead and tell me already," Reggie B. said, situating himself in the recliner and reaching for the popcorn. He'd come over for our standing date: Wednesday night 'Sex & The City' reruns. "I'm already two shades of envy green over you getting to go the BET Awards after-party up in New York this weekend. What happened? Meet any of my favorite celebrities? Dish girl, dish!"

"Yeah, I met Angela Bassett, Gina Price Bythewood, Queen Latifah...whole bunch of folks but the one that left the biggest impression was 'Renzo," I began.

"Who the heck is 'Renzo? Is he another Jamaican rapper?" Reggie B. asked cocking his head to the side. "I think I heard his new song. It goes like..."

"Actually it's Lorenzo. Just rolls right off the tongue, doesn't it? Lorenzo," I said smiling uncontrollably. "I call him 'Renzo though, so he knows it's me calling. But let me tell you, Reggie B., this man is as good looking as the name suggests. He is a bona fide BMW, not a rapper. Stats: He's a Financial Analyst. He's a homeowner. He's no one's baby daddy. And to top it off, he's a lengthy 6'3' hunk of man waiting to be climbed! Whew!"

"Okay. Okay. Calm it down," Reggie B. replied. "I get it. You met a new guy this weekend."

"Not just a guy. The one."

"Girl, please. You always say that."

"I do not!" I spouted back tossing a throw pillow at him.

"You do!" he said batting it away.

"I have said it before, I admit that…but I don't always say it and this time, I really mean it. Lorenzo is it!"

"Don't make me do it," Reggie B. warned.

"Do what?"

"All right little Miss. A quick trip down broken heart lane, it is. Let's start with…there are so many," he said settling his chin on his hand like he was pondering the greatest mysteries of the Bible. "…but I'm going to go with bachelor extraordinaire Wilson Jefferson."

"Oh, that was…"

"It was pure B.S. that man fed you," he finished. "He used his job as an excuse for not committing. But you couldn't see any of that 'cause you were sprung over that man after ya'll had your first date and he whipped that magic stick on you."

"Correction. I whipped it on him and as far as the job thing, well you and I both know teachers don't make that much money."

"Let's be real Sasha. All the teachers we had growing up were married. It's possible to support a wife on a teacher's salary."

"Well…"

"Well nothing," he said, tossing a handful of popcorn into his mouth. "Didn't you ever notice how that high yella sucka turned green every time you mentioned kids? You pushed the issue so much, always saying you wanted to have your first within the first two years of marriage, it's a wonder he stuck around as long as he did."

"He's a teacher. He liked kids."

"He taught high school. Twelfth grade history. The man wasn't dealing with kids."

"Point taken."

"Then after him, it was Benjamin. He wasn't even around long enough for me to catalog his last name in my mind."

"Oh my God. Reggie B., you promised you wouldn't bring him up again. That was so embar..."

"Oh my God is right. *I* was closer to being hetero than *that* man."

"Reggie B..."

"And you, poor thing, just swore up and down that he couldn't be gay 'cause he was so built and because he was a construction worker."

"I still don't think he was gay. I just think..."

"First of all, did the Village People not teach you anything? We're everywhere. There's no specific trade or look for gay men. Second, I don't even know if he realized he was gay. But maybe you're right. Maybe he wasn't gay...but he sure as hell wasn't heterosexual or bisexual, asexual...maybe.

"Reginald Bauer!"

"What? That man was off!"

"Okay. I'll give you that, but I was young," I argued.

"And you haven't grown up much since," he challenged.

"I have!"

"Jason, Michael, Gerald, Hassan, Troy, Justin..."

"Justin really could have been the one but he was right," I said. "I'm focused on my career, and with the demands of *his* job it wouldn't have worked."

"Believe what you want but when two people are truly in love, they make it work."

"Turing into Dr. Phil are ya? It's not always that easy."

"I didn't say it was easy to make it work but folks do," he replied. "And I'll give you partial credit on him because the job was a big issue. I thought he was going to be the one for you too, but then you started being you to the tenth power and that was that?"

"What's that supposed to mean?" I asked turning down the volume as the Sex and the City opening came on.

"It means that you were too eager," he replied emphatically.

"What? I'm never..."

"You always are," he countered. "You act as if their needs are more important than yours. You want a relationship, but you allow them to turn you into nothing more than a booty call. You basically try to force a relationship to develop from attractions that really aren't that strong to begin with anyway. They throw some lines at you about how into you they are; and even if you are not that into them you try to make them into your hubby, which is ridiculous to start with. Then because they're interested, supposedly, you open yourself up to them. That's when they know they got you and they start acting a fool 'til they get tired and just quit you. You act as though you can't see the pattern even though it happens time and time again."

"Well all that's in the past," I replied. "Lorenzo is a totally different guy than all of them. I feel like this one could work."

"I'm not saying it won't," he said shrugging his shoulders. "I'm just saying that if you want different results than what you've been getting, you've got to stop doing the same thing you've been doing in all your other failed relationships."

"I'm not going to stop being me, Reggie B. I..."

"I'm not saying you should. I would never suggest that." Reggie B. began. "You go into relationships the same woman you always are. And that's good..."

"Well, I'm glad to know you acknowledge that I'm doing something right," I teased.

"The trouble is," Reggie B. continued, rolling his eyes, "when you're envisioning yourself with all these men you keep meeting, you never see the full picture; parts of it are more vivid than others and it's always the parts that you *want* to see, never the parts—which always have to do with the man and what he wants, or in most cases, doesn't want—that would ruin the vision you have for you and the guy. But that's where you get in trouble. If you would just look closer at you..."

"I hear you. I just don't think it's as simple as you paint it. You don't know what these men have told me. I don't tell you everything, you know."

"I know..."

"But still, your dating scene is entirely different than mine. I love you Reggie B. but I really don't think you're the one to be giving advice on this."

"Please. I have friends who date men, who date women, and who date both. And you know what? It's all the same. The signs may surface differently but in the long run, they're all the same when someone's not looking to take the relationship in the same direction."

"It's just different when it's a..."

"That's just it. It's not," he interjected. "And I know what you're thinking."

"I'm not thinking anything," I replied.

"You are. I can see it," he said, studying my face. "But the fact is I do date. I face the same issues as you. Hell, I used to be like you but you know what? I learned I had to slow things down and get to know the dudes before I went balls out ga-ga over them."

"Well, you don't seem all that happy to me on the relationship front if we're talking truth."

"Oh, so now you want to make this about me?" he asked, leaning back and to the side in the recliner. "Not happening. You're the one with issues. I've worked through mine."

"Reggie B., I..."

"Naw. I'm good," he said, fixing his hat as he stood up. "But you know what? Maybe you're just one of those people who has to get her heart broken a zillion times before you'll learn. If that's who you want to be, so be it. I'm your friend so I'll be there, but for tonight, I'm through. I'll see you tomorrow."

"Now approaching Pentagon City. Pentagon City is the next stop." I heard an announcer say over the P.A. system. Surprised that I'd been daydreaming the entire ride, I looked around and noticed that the urine man was gone. A young woman and her toddler were now sitting beside me.

"Excuse me," I said standing up. "This is my stop." The woman smiled and turned sideways so I could pass by. As I stepped out of the train, I started scanning the crowd for Reggie B. I finally spotted him waiting at the entrance to the mall.

"The weirdest thing happened today," I said walking up to him.

"Has to do with work, doesn't it?" he asked, smiling smugly.

"Yeah. How'd you guess?"

"I knew it. I knew it!"

"What? What do you know?" I asked.

"I knew that was you that called in on the radio show. Mad Michelle. It was you!" he shouted.

"Was not. Hello! I was producing," I said smacking him on the arm playfully.

"So. You do have a cell phone," he reasoned, raising his eyebrow in disbelief.

"It wasn't me!"

"Oh, God!" he shouted grabbing his heart and falling back on the wall.

"You're so over-dramatic. What?"

"You mean to tell me there's more than one woman running 'round the city giving up the goodies in vain? Damn shame!"

## *Analysis*

By allowing the dust to settle after you first approach a relationship, you are able to see just what it is you have. Because we have not been specifically trained how to have rewarding and successful relationships, we have developed survival skills that tend to get us immediate results with no long term pay-off—as reflected by our national divorce rate and the "lonely heart" population. We have a natural urge to be connected to one another and the ineffective practices of our current society have left us ill-equipped to sustain the relationships we so desire. We find ourselves becoming frustrated with partners that expect from us whatever it was that we offered them in an effort to lure them. The goal seems to be conquest rather than contact.

We have been conditioned to the mind set of acquiring, not appreciating. *Acquiring* is motivated by the ego, which boasts: "Look at me, look what I can do". But when you *appreciate* someone or something, it is a spiritual experience. In this spiritual place, you have a sense of gratitude and amazement at having found such a fulfilling connection with another person. It leaves you with a sense of eternity because you know that such a pleasure will have an everlasting impact and effect on you.

Sasha is allowing herself to be placed in the role of victim because it suits her needs. She is permitting herself to be used sexually because she thinks it will give her an advantage in the relationship. She is trying to create a bond sexually that she has not created emotionally. This is a manipulation tactic that most people use subconsciously, and when it is ineffective, they then feel "victimized". But they're not the victim; they just played the game and lost.

The truth of the matter is that sexual experiences have the potential to be mutually satisfying and if you allow yourself to be deprived of satisfaction, that is a choice that you made and must accept. Now, if the two people involved are sexually gratified, is one person the victim in this encounter? But this is not the real issue. The real issue is that people misuse and abuse sex and then cry wounded soldier when it does not render them the results that they desire. Why is it referred to as "making love" when in fact the people participating are not in love? We call sexual partners "lovers" when in fact, more times than not, the partners don't even really *like* one another, they are just convenient for each other. If we have the desire to share this physical experience with another, why is it not important enough for us to experience it with someone where the words "making love" or "lover" match the actions?

Integrity should always be your primary objective because when you operate in integrity, you operate in order, and with this paradigm, you will never be disappointed. We are lovers because we love one another, but we also use that word when words are not enough and we find ourselves wanting to get so close to another that words seem inadequate. You find yourself wanting your spirit to express, through the vehicle of your body, the things you feel that words just can't articulate. Sounds powerful? Well that is how it was intended to be. Anything less than that is a mere facsimile and as you know there is never any real value in an imitation. Think about it: when people want to keep you away from something valuable, they will sometimes detour you with fear. So I ask you to observe the lives of the people that are attempting to steer you away from this concept by telling you how corny and unrealistic it is. Are they people that are qualified to give you advice, based on the results they have in their lives? And if *you* are the one that is deterring yourself from this concept, take a mental inventory of your life and then ask your self: "Have my past course of action rendered me the results that I desired?

The times when you find yourself not in relationship with another is time that would be more effectively used to prepare yourself for what it is that you desire. In other words, use your "between-relationship" time to work on becoming a better, more evolved YOU. A relationship should not be a completion of self, but a joining of like minds in like places so that the experience can be appreciated and enjoyed together. "Project or pity partners" are not about balance. You know the sort. The project partners are the ones that you try to change to make into who you want, and the pity partners are the ones where you say, "Oh he's nice; he's doing the best he can". Well, neither of these types of relationships is about you being a kind person; they are about you being a fear-based and doubt-ful person in a disguise of goodwill. You stay in these relation-ships because you don't believe that you can do better. That is what these people usually serve to show you.

But knowing what you want and realizing that you are not yet equipped to get it allows you the opportunity to get your-self ready. You can become whatever it is you desire to be because the truth of the matter is that you are already what-ever you want to be; you just have to remind yourself of this fact and operate in that awareness. It is like long-lost royalty: they are royals whether they are aware of it or not, but when they become aware, they are trained to operate appropriately in the role of their birthright. Not knowing who they really were did not change the fact of their being royal; it just hin-dered them from behaving as a royal.

We have to learn the difference between who we *are* and what we *do*. We *do* things because of our opinions and views, but those things don't make us who we *are*, they are us just expressing what we feel at the time. Who you are never changes, but what you feel and what you do can and will change. If Sasha were to change her outlook on life, she would not have the need to put the needs of others ahead of herself to her own detriment. She is a female and is a soothing per-son, and that just does not change because her views change. She is a spiritual being, and *that* won't change because her views change. Get the picture? Anything that can change based on an opinion, viewpoint or belief is not who you are.

When you don't like your behavior patterns, peel the onion that is *you* and discover what the motivation is behind those patterns; then find an alternative method of operation. Usually, at the core of ineffective behaviors there is a false belief that needs to be dispelled. Once you identify this erroneous thought, you can replace it with truth, and your behavior will automatically begin to change because you will no longer subscribe to the belief you previously had. This in turn, dissolves the needs that supported that old, ineffective behavior.

Now, this is a simple process as long as you are willing to be honest with yourself and to call a spade a spade. Your desire cannot be to make yourself look good or to make excuses for your behaviors or choices. It makes no sense to disapprove of an action when someone else does it, and when you do it, feel justified because of your situation. You will only impede your progress by adopting this posture. If your real goal is to be successful in your development of new behavioral patterns, you must start with the person you see in the mirror. When you deal with him or her, you will find that everything else will be forced to change position because you have changed yours. You can't just say that you want different results; you have to bring those results about by allowing the process to happen through you. Faith without works is dead. What this means is that you have to think it, operate in it, and then reap the rewards from it. It is easy to say it and not do it, but this will never produce results, even though it sounds good.

Allow yourself to fall in love with what *is*, not with what you think *can* be. This will prove to be a more effective approach to relationships of every kind.

# 14. Conclusion

By now, this should be clear to you: we have to respect each other and allow each other to have our own journeys. By allowing someone else to have his or her journey, you don't have to become a sacrificial lamb to their personal evolution. Rather, look at the situation as a learning experience for them and for yourself. Realize the things that happened in your life are guiding you, preparing you for what's to come.

Recognize and respect the signs that you have grown, and that you now have no need to be tied to things that don't serve your greater good. It is like a pair of shoes that no longer fit you: when you outgrow them, it is in your best interest and health for you to get rid of them. By giving them away, you relieve yourself of the discomfort of the experience and you make room for a newer, more suitable pair that will actually fit, and fit well. Now, this does not mean that you don't, or didn't like those old shoes. On the contrary, you like them, that's why you bought them, and you hate to give them up because now they are familiar. But know that you can appreciate something and also release it for your greater good, making room for something greater to enter. How exciting is *that*?

You will find that it is easier to make room for your greater good to enter and for you to more effortlessly move on your journey, when you accept that there are no victims and no perpetrators. When you place yourself in victim mode, you look for ways to prove that you are being taken advantage of—which is the same thing as saying you played no role in what happened to you. This method of operation keeps you feeling victimized and gives you an excuse to feel sorry for yourself. That is all well and good if your goal is to stay stuck in "stupid" and "stagnated". While you are being the victim, you are creating an environment of fear and negativity, and this will keep you paralyzed and impede your progress. You must maintain the belief that everything that happens to you happens for your good, an opportunity for you to get a lesson or a blessing. If you are able to see what good the experience brought to your life and focus on that, you can then ignore what you believe that it took away from your life; and you will no longer feel like being the victim. You will create for yourself a spirit of gratitude, and in that gratitude you will be able to see and receive blessings beyond your wildest imagination.

What about when you find yourself coupled with someone who promised you things but did not "deliver", someone of whom you can say that their character was something other than what they demonstrated, or they contradicted their words with their actions? Know that this person has not successfully conquered his/her relationship issues or patterns sufficiently enough to be a good partner for you at this time; and for your sake and theirs, don't keep them in a situation that you know is sure to fail. Set them free to continue on their journey to being who they desire to be—and continue your own journey without them. Don't use your gifts to try to render results from another that he or she is incapable of giving. The key is to be able to identify this as quickly as possible and move on. Maya Angelou has said, "When someone shows you who they are the first time, believe them". We have to respect relationships enough to allow them to serve their purpose and grow from them. Let them go if they are not a good fit.

When you know your worth, you will find yourself less likely to rationalize away unproductive behaviors. You will see the signs that the other person is simply not ready to be in your space and you will realize that that person is on their journey, same as you. And although they may desire to be at a certain stage in their life, they are not there yet, and it is not your place to get them there. Recognize when you are not equally yoked, and move on.

Know that the power is not in your *control* but in your *release*, and when you let go of things you make room for other things. Don't delude your self into manipulating, calculating and strategizing to make a relationship work, because it should not be that hard. Know that the signs are always there; you just have to heed them.

Women, especially, often stay too long in bad relationships. Men, even though they don't usually say it with words, will exit a bad relationship mentally (if not physically) when they pick up on the signs. Ladies, this is a lesson that will serve you well to learn quickly. Sometimes your partner just won't know how to say goodbye, so save them the trouble and do it for them. You will save yourself a lot of heartache, and in the long run, it doesn't matter who says it first when both of you know when the situation is not working, so don't wait until it has beaten you both down.

Remember, you can't get where you're going by staying where you're at. You have to shed the old to accept the new. It's not easy, but we tend to hold onto nothing and try and make it something, because we're afraid of what's to come. Not only will you get better at picking people who are a better fit for you, but when they're not a good enough fit, you will get out of it faster and with less pain.

A word of caution to women: We have been given the gifts of nurturing, teaching, and patience. These virtues have been placed in us for the purpose of child-rearing. But a lot of the time, we apply them in the wrong context in order to compensate for a man's shortcomings. Our impulse or inclination is to use these gifts with our romantic partner as if he was our child, and we overlook flaws. But he is not your child, he is supposed to be your partner and your equal. And there is a big difference between *supporting* one's partner and trying to *save* one's partner. "Mothering" your partner is a self-defeating practice that is unfair to you *and* your partner. It is not your duty to raise grown folk. The only real reason that you do it is because you don't believe that you are worthy of a man that is perfectly suited for what you desire, so you engage in trying to "build" a man; you decide to just work with whatever you have in front of you. This, I guarantee you, is a formula for failure. (But you already new that. Didn't you?)

So what can you do to begin to change? The first step to develop is the ability to spot the **Representative**. The Representative is the other person's best "Me" ever. It's the person they are showing you—who may or may not be anything like the *real* person underneath.

When someone shows you their Representative, it is because they think that their regular "Me" is not good enough. So they introduce you to the "Me" that they want to be, but have not quite achieved, and usually it is all down hill from that initial contact. This person is not yet able to actually BE their Representative, so signs of the real "Me" will start seeping through.

But that is when it is up to you to love and respect yourself enough to realize that if you were attracted to the Representative, then that is who you agreed to engage in relationship with; and when the Representative exits, then you should exit as well. If you don't, then you begin to date someone you don't even know, thereby subjecting yourself to behaviors that you are not willing to accept. It is not what he/she did in the past, it is what they are currently doing *now*, because yesterday is gone and tomorrow is not promised to you, so today is all you have. And for those of you who are looking for an excuse to continue in your self-destructive behavior patterns, know that it is not "abandoning someone when times get hard" when you decide to leave someone you know is not a good fit for you. You know in your heart of hearts if this person is truly showing you who they really are. Allow your internal navigational system to guide you. Listen to it, and don't rationalize away the warning signs.

Remember that people, by and large, are not maliciously going after you. They are just trying to get their own needs met and are playing out their desire to be their authentic self. They don't have what it takes to keep up, to make the choice to put in the energy to be their authentic selves, even though at some level they genuinely *want* to be. When the behavior patterns begin to change and if you don't like what you see, realize that this is simply not the relationship for you. Whatever motivated the person to show you their very best "Me" is no longer there. It's just that simple, so bless the experience and move on to your greater blessing.

A relationship is supposed to be a peaceful, complimentary coexistence, not a high or a hiding place. Most of us use our relationships as fixes for whatever else isn't going well. We are drawn to relationships with others so that we don't have to deal with other unresolved issues in ourselves. But relating with someone effectively and maturely can give you a partner on the journey of life. Allow yourself to mature in the area of relationships and enjoy the marvels that life has for you from a healthy place. Cast your fear aside. Be present and partake of the gift that sharing, caring and authenticity can bring.

We are constantly talking about our problems, dealing with the symptoms instead of treating the cause. We are a mentally lazy people—not to say that we are not intelligent, because for years we have been identifying the problems, but where we drop the ball is in our refusal to take action. We fear that taking action in a new direction will also take us out of our comfort zone, but in order to grow you have to stretch, and stretching is uncomfortable at first. But what emerges at the end of the metamorphosis is much more beautiful than the beginning product—it's like the caterpillar and the butterfly.

I hope that this book will give you the food for thought to nourish yourself in new and better ways, so that you will be strong enough to embrace your authentic self and receive the gift that a healthy relationship has for you. Don't be afraid to shed your "faces of sickness" to walk in your greatness.

# Tools and Resources

Thank you for joining me on this miraculous journey. Here are just a few of the powerful programs we have developed at NuMe Enterprises, as well as other resources that will support you in continuing the work you have started with this book. I invite you to visit my web site at www.NuMeEnterprises.com to learn more about our workshops, products, and other resources to support you in creating your life plan and becoming all that you are meant to be!

## *Exposure Workshop and Retreat*

This is a wonderful combination of workshop and retreat, where the mind is exposed to new concepts that will raise your level of awareness while the body is completely pampered and guided to become centered on a state of peace within, the goal being to create a state of wellness. This 3-day workshop was designed specifically for women, structured to assist them in discovering new ways to achieve their goals effortlessly as well as to understand and appreciate who they are, resulting in a silent demand for respect.

## *"I like Me"—Day Camp for Kids*

A camp experience like no other! This one week summer camp for girls, grades 6–8, exposes pre-teens and young teens to information and tools to assist them in making the transition from little girls into young adulthood. The camp consists of amazing workshops designed specifically for this age group to help them discover and appreciate who they are, to understand their insecurities, and to prepare them to embark on the journey of maturation. In conjunction with the workshops, there are modules on make-up application, hip/hop dance, yoga, etiquette and much more.

## The Power to Change Tour

The Power to Change Tour is a call to action. It is for anyone who believes that there is no way to break the cycle of dysfunctional and diminishing behaviors. Unlike any other motivational or self-help series, it identifies the problems and provides audiences with much needed solutions and tools necessary to achieve miraculous results.

## Financial Empowerment—The debt free millionaire movement

Learn important techniques that will change your life forever. You will be shown how to participate in the abundance of life that is there for the partaking. Tai will reveal financial secrets that will empower and create wealth in your life. The information is simple and easy to apply and is guaranteed to create results that will astound and amaze you. Learn how to let your money work hard for you instead of you working hard for your money. Conquer your problems with debt, create additional sources of income, and much more.

## Small Change Leads To BIG Things—The Africa Project NuMe

Tai Archbold has a project that is near and dear to her heart, where through her non profit division, she raises funds in conjunction with American school children to assist African school children with their academic careers. Contact Tai to find out more about this important work and how YOU can contribute and make a difference!

## *Recommended Reading List*

- Take Five, The Five Minute Fix For Transforming Your Life by Tai Archbold
- *Excuse Me, Your Life Is Waiting by Lynn Grabhorn*
- *Radical Forgiveness* by Colin Tippin
- The Little Soul and the Sun by Neale Donald Walsh

# About Tai

Tai Archbold was born in West Palm Beach, Florida, and is the oldest of four children. A great portion of Tai's childhood years were spent in Nassau, Bahamas. Exposure to island mentality and the powerful influence of her Bahamian grandmother (a career Registered Nurse employed in the mental health industry) cultivated her dimensional perspectives of life. At a young age, family and friends labeled Tai as anything but ordinary. Unlike other children, she noticed manipulation, miscommunication, infidelity, unrest, struggle, and misplaced acceptance within society. This was the beginning of the revelation of her intended life purpose.

Tai's journey led her to study Rehabilitative Services; concentrating on Behavior Modification. A special major graduate of California State University, Los Angeles, she received a Bachelor of Science in the program that she designed and introduced into the California State University System. Tai's portfolio includes experience as a Behavior Modification Specialist in the fields of substance abuse, parenting, relationships, and family modeling. She also worked as a Federal Covert Investigator for the Women, Infants, and Children program.

Aside from her professional experience, Tai has spent her life on a mission of observation in pursuit of understanding the human position in an effort to make existence better. She often states, "Don't just tell me what to do, teach me how to do it". Disgusted with a lifetime of personal dysfunctional and manipulative behaviors, Tai embarked on a mission of re-birth. To date, the culmination of her life experiences has created an enlightened state of being within her that she shares with her audiences.

"Eyes Wide Open, Mind Shut Tight: Exploring Relationship Issues and Uncovering the Power to Change" is the vehicle by which she delivers her observations, opinions, and passions. The time is right for change because people desperately need it and most importantly they want it.

Currently, Tai spreads her time between Atlanta, Georgia and Los Angeles, California, raising her two very talented children and fulfilling God's purpose for her life.

# Eyes Wide Open, Minds Shut Tight, *The Series*

This powerful series of books helps the reader to lay a foundation for living, one which facilitates understanding and raises the level of consciousness that leads to change, and provides tools that you can use with directions that work. It's your choice how and when you will use what is available to you. How uncomfortable are you where you are right now? Are you uncomfortable enough to make a change?

This book is for those who truly desire change in their lives and are willing to open their minds to the thoughts and truths that their eyes have seen for a life time. New results require new actions, and new actions require a mind open to truth without fear. I know that what I have learned and experienced on my life's journey will make your journey easier. Come and let me share my approach with you. Remove the chains that restrict your thinking and that limit your ability to connect with yourself. Don't fake the experience, live the experience for real. Own it, practice it and receive the rewards from it. It's already available to you right now, take the leap and experience the joy!

978-0-595-41458-1
0-595-41458-3